MC
Book-of-the-Month Club, Inc.

Dear Fellow Book Lover,

About nine months ago I was browsing through the catalogue of a small publishing company, Ecco Press. And I came upon a book by a writer I have always admired, Betty Fussell. The Book-of-the-Month Club had just taken Ms. Fussell's wonderful new cookbook, I Hear America Cooking. So I was naturally curious about the Ecco Press book Eating In, which has as its subtitle The Pocket Cookbook. It's that all right, but a lot more. As I read through it, I was enchanted by its style and its surprising dimensions—its recipes for easy cooking, its shopping tips, its suggestions on which wine to serve with specific meals. I thought to myself, what a nice gift this would make for our members. And here it is.

This is simply one small way for us to thank you for being a part of the Book-of-the-Month family, and for your support of the Club and what it stands for.

Good reading to you always.

Sincerely,

Al Silverman
Chairman

AS:woo

EATING IN

BETTY FUSSELL

Wine Selections by
Joshua Wesson and
William Wadsworth

THE ECCO PRESS
NEW YORK

Published by The Ecco Press in 1986
18 West 30 Street, New York, NY 10001

Published simultaneously in Canada by
Penguin Books Canada Ltd.
2801 John Street, Markham, Ontario, Canada L3R 1B4

Printed in the United States of America

Library of Congress Cataloguing in Publication Data
    Fussell, Betty Harper
    Eating in.
    Includes index
    1. Cookery for two.   I. Title.
    Tx652.F88   1986   641.5'61   86-6203
    ISBN 0-88001-125-4

    Illustrations by Angeline Acain and Tucky Fussell
    Cover and Book Design by Beth Tondreau

CONTENTS

Key to recipe symbols:

 major ingredient

 suggested accompaniment

wine recommendation

alternative recipe

INTRODUCTION

This book is designed for the person who enjoys good food and good wine but who is more used to eating out than eating in. We all know the need for a lift at the end of a long, hard day, but shopping and cooking sound like work—more work than fighting for a cab, waiting at the bar, shouting over the din, surviving the memory test of the waiter's specials and the size of the waiter's bill.

Here is a pocket guide you can slip into your jacket or purse to make shopping and cooking less like work and more like a pleasurable and practical alternative to eating out. With this book in hand, you don't need to plan ahead. You can shop for food and wine on the way home from work and know that you will have a meal on the table, the candles lit, the stereo humming, within the hour.

Most of the dishes and their variants can be served as one-dish and often one-pan meals. They call for the simplest of fresh ingredients that can be prepared by the simplest of methods to provide something special that will perk up your appetite and excite your sense of adventure. Hungry we all are, but satisfied we are often not. Here you will find old friends in new alliances, familiar comforts invigorated by the unexpected—scallops with a sprinkling of sesame oil, rice made creamy with yogurt, tuna delicately smoked with tea leaves and herbs. . . .

SHOPPING

To help you shop, each recipe in the book highlights the major ingredients. These are ingredients that you will most likely have to shop for. A basic larder is assumed, so staples like butter, olive oil, vinegar, dry spices, onion, garlic, lemons, milk, flour, sugar and eggs are not highlighted. Remember that seasonings, herbs, and spices can be changed, depending on what the market or your larder provides.

To make shopping easy, make it personal. Establish a network of local specialists who can greet you by name and who will give you their best because you're a regular. Patronize your local Asian produce store, the Italian fish market, the German butcher, the Jewish baker. Insist on quality and be ready to pay for it. Remember that for the price of an ordinary meal eating out, you can be extravagant eating in. Eating in is the time to indulge in a whole black truffle or two, a little caviar, a quail, a chocolate naughty from the pastry shop, a sumptuous bottle of wine.

With your pocket guide in hand, start at the produce counter and choose your meal by what's fresh and ripe. If the avocados are granite hard, don't try Avocado-Pineapple Cream tonight. Buy the avocado today for use next week. In the same way, the pineapple should be yellow, not green. The melons should smell of melons at their stem end. The pears, mangoes, and papayas should yield to gentle pressure in the palm of the hand. Even in summer the tomatoes should be scrutinized with care for perfect ripeness.

Fresh herbs can bring a dish to life; now that they are more available, try new ways of using them. If you have none at home, remember to buy a couple of yellow onions, a bunch of green onions, a head of garlic, a few lemons and limes, for these are the staples of the recipes herein.

Now that fish has become pricier than meat, choose your fishman with care. If you see counters of fish with sunken eyes, tanks of lethargic lobsters and floating trout, choose a new fishman. When buying fillets, ask to see the underside. When buying whole fish, look for clear, bulging eyes, red gills, and firm flesh. Don't just look—poke your finger in the flesh, and if it doesn't spring back, don't buy it.

Find a butcher who will cut meat to your measure and won't sneer when you demand veal scallops as thin as paper or a fresh duck, quartered. Cellophane-wrapped meat, fowl, or fish is always a gamble because you can't see the underside, nor can you smell or touch.

Since many city stores now carry good fresh-baked loaves of bread—French baguettes, Italian semolina, Jewish pumpernickel and rye—you may not have to seek out the baker in his shop. Good pastry, however, may require a trip to the best pâtisserie you can find. Because the desserts in this book are limited to fruits and the simplest of tarts or chocolate creams, a bought dessert is a good place for an extravagant outlay in the exchange of money for time.

Good fresh pasta is everywhere, and you can experiment with colors and kinds. If your mood is for a light creamy sauce, choose a fettuccine or similar egg noodle. If you yearn for a heartier sauce of olives, anchovies, and tomatoes, you will need the heft of a dried pasta, such as De Cecco.

For the recipes in this book, you need but a small larder of oil, vinegar, butter, seasonings, herbs, and spices, but they should be the best you can reasonably buy. Keep two olive oils: a fine extra-virgin French or Italian oil such as Colavita for salads, and a gutsy Greek, Portuguese, or Spanish oil, such as Goya, for cooking.

With vinegars, buy three. Buy first an Italian balsamic, such as Fini, which will prove as useful in sauces as Worcestershire and far more subtle. Then buy a pair of good wine vinegars, one red and one white, which you can replenish with heel-taps of last night's wine, according to color.

For these recipes:

Butter always means unsalted. Land O'Lakes is a good commercial brand, but you can make a meal of butter and bread if you splurge on a sweet Normandy butter imported from France.

Cream means heavy, unless specified as half-and-half or crème fraîche. You can buy crème fraîche for a price or make it ahead by mixing 1 cup heavy cream with ½ cup sour cream and letting it stand at room temperature overnight. It will keep, refrigerated, for about a week.

Eggs mean standard large eggs.

Lemon juice means freshly squeezed.

Salt means sea salt.

Black pepper means freshly ground, as does nutmeg.

Fresh gingerroot can be easily grated if you peel it and keep it tightly wrapped in plastic in the freezer.

When buying dried herbs or spices, search out an ethnic spice shop—East Indian stores are especially good—and buy them in the smallest quantity possible. When you can, buy whole spices, such as seeds, pods, bark, and leaves, and grind them as needed in a blender or coffee grinder just before use. Among packaged brands, the Spice Market and Spice Islands are reputable. Because prolonged heat and light destroy the taste of dried herbs, keep them tightly sealed in a cool, dark cupboard or in the refrigerator or freezer.

Dried herbs and spices will release the most flavor if you heat them in a dry skillet just before using.

COOKING

Your cooking equipment can be as minimal as your larder. You do need a skillet with a well-fitting lid. The best skillet is one that, once properly seasoned with oil, will be permanently stick-free, such as heavy cast iron, or an impermeable nonstick type, such as Calphalon. The most versatile skillet is a wok with a lid, because it can sauté, deep-fry, smoke, or steam with a minimal amount of heat, oil, or liquid.

Any kind of oven will do, except a microwave. You should always allow 10 minutes to preheat.

You need one good sharp knife and a ceramic or steel sharpener to keep it that way. Although a variety of size and cutting edge in knives is convenient—such as a serrated bread knife or tomato slicer—one good knife will do the work of twenty if you keep it sharp and are used to working with it. A Chinese cleaver can be as flexible as a French chef's knife if you get the feel of it.

If you want a few pieces of specialized equipment, buy a citrus-peel shredder for scraping orange and lemon rind, and a time-saving spin-dryer for salad greens.

Everybody needs a blender, for puréeing, grinding, frothing, and emulsifying. If possible, buy a food processor, which can do things the blender can't and which will save you time and labor.

You don't need a battery of heavy cookbooks. One encyclopedic reference such as *The Joy of Cooking* will tell you how to make a mayonnaise or roast a turkey.

Before beginning a recipe, you do need to read it through to see what's required. Do you need to pre-heat the oven? Do you have the major ingredients? Do you have the time? Do you have the yen?

EATING

Today we don't think in terms of three-course meals of soup, entrée, and dessert. We are more health-conscious than ever, but we know that we don't have to balance each meal or each day, as long as we balance the week. One night we may graze on a salad of hydroponic lettuce and on the next gorge on lobster and chocolate truffles. Liberated from the culinary rules of our forefathers, we can eat what appeals at the moment and be nourished by the variety and quality of the ingredients.

Although most of the main dishes are designed to be complete meals, I have added a few starters, companions, and finishers to add to variety and flexibility when you want a little something more. For me, a crusty bread, a fresh green salad, and a fine ripe fruit turns a main dish into a meal that satisfies, whether I'm eating alone or with a friend, but I've included with each recipe a suggestion for some food that complements or contrasts.

The quantities of these recipes are designed for two because it is easier to shop and cook for two than for one. Usually I count on ½ pound of meat, fish, or fowl per person, and ¼ pound of pasta. Obviously you can scale this down or increase it to suit your appetite. Just as obviously, you can multiply quantities to cook for four or eight, or divide to cook for one. Cooking for two, however, even when eating alone, has the virtue of providing leftovers. Most of the dishes here are as good at room temperature or chilled as they are hot. Some are even better reheated. One thing to keep in mind: if you plan to use the dish cold, use olive oil instead of butter.

Although I've streamlined these recipes for speed and ease of shopping, preparing, and cooking, eating is another matter. Eating is less the means than the reward for surviving yet another day, for suffering the subway or freeway, the erratic boss, the jangling telephone, and the frenzied pace. Eating, by contrast, should be luxuriously slow. Eating in, you don't have to worry about staying sober, grabbing a cab, or paying the bill. You've already paid. You can swirl the wine in your glass and drink deeply. You can linger over the smoky taste of the roasted peppers, the toothsomeness of the fresh pasta, the creaminess of the coconut curry, the smell of that perfectly ripe peach. You are home, thank God, eating in.

STARTERS

ROASTED PEPPER SALAD

- ■ 2 sweet red peppers
- ■ 2 small zucchini
- ■ 1 small bunch fresh spinach
- ■ ¼ pound Monterey Jack or Muenster cheese
- ■ ¼ pound feta cheese, drained and rinsed
- ☐ 2 teaspoons balsamic vinegar
- ☐ ⅓ cup olive oil
- ☐ Salt and black pepper

Char the skins of the red peppers under a broiler or directly over a gas flame. Put the peppers in a paper bag to steam for 5 minutes. Remove the skins, stems, and seeds. Cut the flesh into strips lengthwise.

Don't peel the zucchini but cut off both ends. Shred the zucchini in a processor, or cut in fine strips lengthwise; then mix with the crumbled feta.

Cut off the spinach stems, wash the leaves well, and spin them dry. Make a bed of the spinach on a serving plate. Arrange the peppers with strips of Monterey Jack cheese in a sunburst pattern on the spinach. Put the zucchini in the middle.

Make a dressing by mixing together the vinegar, oil, and seasonings and pour over the salad.

FRIED GORGONZOLA

- ■ ½ pound Gorgonzola cheese, chilled
- ■ ½ cup walnuts, finely chopped
- ■ 1 cup fresh bread crumbs
- ☐ 1 egg, beaten
- ☐ Oil for deep frying
- ■ Chicory leaves

Remove the rind from the cheese and cut the cheese into 1-inch cubes. Mix the walnuts with the bread crumbs.

Dip the cheese cubes in the egg and then roll in the walnut mixture.

Heat the oil until hot but not smoking, and fry the cubes a few at a time. Drain on paper towels and serve on a bed of chicory.

FRESH POTATO CHIPS

- ■ 4 cups vegetable oil or lard
- ■ 2 Idaho baking potatoes
- ☐ Salt, black pepper, and cayenne pepper

Heat 1 to 2 inches of oil in a wok or deep skillet. Scrub the potatoes well but don't peel them. Cut them into thin slices (⅛ inch thick) in a food processor or by hand and pat them dry with paper towels.

When the oil is hot but not smoking (when a test slice of potato bubbles and floats on the top), add the potatoes a few slices at a time (to keep the oil hot) until they go limp. Remove with a slotted spoon and drain on paper towels. Let the slices rest for 10 minutes or more.

Reheat the oil and refry the slices until they are crisp and browned, 2 to 4 minutes. Drain again on paper towels and season to taste. Eat immediately.

TAPENADE DIP

- ■ Raw vegetables (carrots, fennel, celery, cauliflower and broccoli flowerets, zucchini, snow peas, etc.)
- ■ ½ cup black Mediterranean olives, pitted
- ☐ 1 garlic clove, mashed
- ☐ 1 tablespoon drained capers
- ■ 4 anchovy fillets
- ☐ 1 egg yolk
- ☐ 1 teaspoon Dijon mustard
- ☐ 1 tablespoon lemon juice
- ☐ ¼ cup olive oil
- ☐ 1 tablespoon chopped fresh basil or parsley, or other herbs

Prepare the vegetables and arrange on a platter. Put the olives, garlic, capers, anchovies, egg, mustard, and lemon juice in a blender and purée until smooth. With the motor running, add the olive oil in a thin stream until it is absorbed by the purée. Put the sauce in a bowl, and garnish with the basil.

Instead of vegetables, use cooked shrimp, broiled sea scallops, or toasted French bread.

PASTA

ANGEL'S HAIR WITH CAVIAR

- ■ ⅓ pound angel's hair pasta (capellini)
- ■ ½ cup fish stock or clam juice
- □ 3 tablespoons butter
- ■ 1 cup crème fraîche or sour cream
- ■ ¼ cup chopped chives
- □ Black pepper
- □ Grated rind of 1 lemon
- ■ 2 ounces sturgeon or golden whitefish caviar

Bring 3 quarts of water (with a tablespoon of salt and a teaspoon of oil) to a boil. Add the pasta, stir well, and cook rapidly. Test after 1 or 2 minutes by forking out a strand and nibbling the end of it. Keep testing until it has the right chewy tenderness—*al dente*—on your teeth.

Meanwhile, in a skillet or saucepan large enough to toss the pasta, bring the stock to a boil and melt the butter in it. Remove from the heat, add the cream and chives, and keep the sauce warm.

Drain the pasta the moment it is done and toss the pasta thoroughly in the sauce. Grind black pepper over the top and sprinkle with the lemon rind and caviar.

■ Serve with a stir-fry of snow peas and slivered sweet red peppers. End with Fresh Fruit Macedonia (p. 116).

Y Caviar always suggests a sparkling wine, though real Champagne isn't absolutely necessary: a sparkling white from the Loire or California is just as appropriate. A bottle of Codorniu from Spain would be another, even less expensive, possibility. If you prefer something without effervescence, try the full-flavored Vernacchia from Italy.

► Angel's hair with mascarpone cheese: Put ½ cup mascarpone in a blender with 3 tablespoons of melted butter and 1 to 2 tablespoons Gorgonzola cheese. Blend with 1½ cups of heavy cream. Season to taste and toss with the cooked pasta. Thin the sauce, if needed, with dry vermouth.

LEMON AND RED PEPPER PASTA

- ☐ 2 tablespoons (¼ stick) butter
- ■ 1 sweet red pepper
- ☐ 1 lemon
- ■ 1 cup heavy cream or crème fraîche
- ☐ Salt, black pepper, and cayenne pepper
- ■ ½ pound fresh fettuccine
- ☐ Grated Parmesan cheese

Bring 3 quarts of water (with a tablespoon of salt and a teaspoon of oil) to a boil.

Meanwhile, prepare the sauce. Melt the butter in a large skillet or saucepan. Quarter the pepper and remove the stem and seeds; then dice the flesh and add it to the skillet. Grate the lemon rind into the skillet and add the juice of half the lemon, the cream, and salt and peppers. Warm the sauce, but keep it well below the simmer.

Add the pasta to the boiling water, test after 1 or 2 minutes, and keep testing until it is *al dente*. Drain immediately and toss the pasta in the sauce. Serve with a bowl of grated Parmesan cheese.

Serve with a watercress salad and follow with Blackened Figs (p. 112).

Lemon and cream with pasta call for a dry white from Italy: Gavi, Orvieto Secco, or, for something slightly more exotic, a Fiano di Avellino. A very dry Chenin Blanc from California might also work well.

► For a different vegetable crunch, add fresh corn kernels and lightly steamed asparagus tips to the same lemon-cream sauce.

Pesto Pasta and Potatoes

PESTO SAUCE
- ■ 1 cup fresh basil leaves, packed
- ■ ¼ cup parsley sprigs
- ☐ ¼ cup olive oil
- ☐ 1 to 2 garlic cloves
- ☐ Pinch of salt
- ☐ ¼ cup pine nuts
- ■ ⅓ cup grated Parmesan cheese (buy 2 ounces for the entire recipe)

PASTA AND POTATOES
- ■ 4 small red new potatoes
- ■ ¼ pound string beans
- ■ 3 green onions (scallions), minced
- ☐ Salt and black pepper
- ■ ½ pound dried pasta (penne, fusilli, farfalle, orecchiette)
- ■ ½ cup grated Parmesan cheese

Make the pesto by puréeing all the sauce ingredients in a blender or processor. If the sauce is too thick to handle, add a tablespoon of soft butter or a little more oil.

Boil the potatoes in their skins until fork-tender, about 10 minutes. Drain and cool; then slice thin.

Trim the beans and boil them until they are no longer "raw" but are still crisp, about 5 to 8 minutes. Drain and set aside. Mix the onions with the beans and potatoes. Season lightly with salt and pepper.

Boil the pasta in 3 quarts of water (with a tablespoon of salt and a teaspoon of oil) until *al dente*. Drain and toss the pasta, potatoes, beans, and onions with the pesto and serve with a bowl of the Parmesan.

Serve with an escarole salad. Finish with a platter of cheese.

A fairly sweet California Riesling will cut the garlic. If you lean toward red, look for a substantial Nebbiolo from northern Italy, such as Ghemme, Spanna, or Gattinara. Even Barolo would be traditionally appropriate.

To make pesto burgers, mix half the pesto with a pound of ground chuck, ground lamb, or a mixture of ground chuck and pork. Add salt and pepper to taste and shape into two large patties. Sauté the patties in a tablespoon *each* of butter and oil to make the patties crusty on the outside but rare within.

SESAME-SCALLOP NOODLES

- ⬛ ⅓ pound egg noodles (fresh is best)
- ⬛ 1 tablespoon sesame oil
- ⬛ ½ pound scallops
- ⬛ 2 tablespoons toasted sesame seeds
- ⬛ 2 green onions (scallions), finely chopped
- ⬛ 3 tablespoons sesame seed paste (tahini) or fresh peanut butter
- ☐ ¼ cup brewed tea
- ☐ 1 tablespoon soy sauce
- ☐ 1 teaspoon sugar
- ☐ 1 teaspoon wine vinegar
- ☐ ½ garlic clove, minced
- ☐ Minced fresh hot pepper, hot red pepper flakes, or cayenne pepper

Boil the fresh noodles in 3 quarts of water (with a tablespoon of salt and a teaspoon of oil) for about 2 minutes or until *al dente*. Drain and rinse with cold water. Drain again and mix in a bowl with 1 teaspoon of the sesame oil.

If using sea scallops, cut them in quarters. Add the remaining sesame oil to a hot wok or skillet and sauté the scallops, turning, about 1 minute. Add to the noodles with the sesame seeds and green onions.

Put the remaining ingredients in a blender to make a sauce. Thin or thicken as desired with more tea or paste. Adjust the hotness to your taste. Toss the noodle mixture in the sauce. Serve at room temperature.

◖ Good with a crunchy green vegetable like snow peas or broccoli.

🍷 The spiciness here is best matched by a semi-sweet white: try a Chenin Blanc from California or a Vouvray Demi-Sec.

▶ For a very different effect, toss the hot noodles and scallops with ½ cup toasted poppy seeds puréed in a blender with 4 tablespoons of melted butter. Season with salt and pepper to taste and serve at once.

LEEK AND ARUGULA FETTUCCINE

- ■ 1 bunch arugula
- ☐ 2 tablespoons (¼ stick) butter
- ■ 2 sprigs fresh mint
- ■ 2 to 3 tablespoons dry vermouth
- ☐ Salt and black pepper
- ■ 2 leeks
- ☐ 2 tablespoons olive oil
- ■ ½ pound fettuccine (or other fresh noodles)

Bring 3 quarts of water (with a tablespoon of salt and a teaspoon of oil) to a boil.

Meanwhile, cut the stems from the arugula and wash the leaves well. Melt the butter in a large skillet and sauté the leaves for 2 or 3 minutes. Put the arugula, mint, vermouth, and salt and pepper in the blender and purée until smooth. Taste for seasoning.

Cut off the roots and tops of the leeks and wash the leeks well. Cut them in half lengthwise and shred finely. Sauté the leeks in the oil until tender but not browned. Add the arugula purée to the leeks and keep the sauce warm.

Add the pasta to the boiling water, test after 1 or 2 minutes, and keep testing until it is *al dente*. Drain immediately and toss the pasta in the sauce.

■ Start with Fried Gorgonzola (p. 3) and finish with a coffee granite or a lemon sorbet.

▮ If you prefer white, look for Pinot Grigio, dry Orvieto, or Tunina. For red, either Chianti Classico, Rubesco, or Ghemme would provide the right combination of full flavor and medium body.

► For pasta with puréed peas and mint, quickly sauté a handful of sugar-snap peas (or snow peas) in 3 tablespoons of butter in a covered skillet. Purée them in a processor with a sprig or two of mint, salt, pepper, and nutmeg; then thin the purée with hot cream and toss with the pasta and some grated Parmesan cheese.

SHELLFISH

Black Pepper Shrimp

- ■ 1½ pounds large raw shrimp in the shell
- □ ¼ pound (1 stick) butter
- □ 2 tablespoons freshly ground black pepper
- □ 2 garlic cloves, minced

Rinse and drain the shrimp and put them in a baking dish in a single layer. Cut the butter into pieces and put them on top of the shrimp. Sprinkle the pepper and garlic over the whole. Bake at 350 degrees for 30 minutes, turning the shrimp once or twice to coat the shells with the butter.

Serve the shrimp with French or Italian bread (and a couple of hot washcloths), because you will peel the shrimp as you go and sop up the butter with hunks of bread.

Accompany the shrimp with a salad you can also eat with your fingers: asparagus spears or endive and arugula. End with coconut ice.

This is a perfect occasion for a good Premier Cru Chablis or Sancerre from France. California Sauvignon

Blanc could be an alternative, or, for a change, try a fino sherry.

► Broil the shrimp (or other shellfish) by dipping them in a mixture of 4 tablespoons *each* melted butter and olive oil. Then roll each piece in a mixture of dried herbs, such as thyme, rosemary, oregano, marjoram, summer savory, or basil. Broil quickly for 3 to 5 minutes, turning the shrimp once. Heat the remaining butter and oil and use as a dipping sauce.

CORN AND SHRIMP BRÛLÉE

- ■ 3 ears sweet corn
- ■ ½ pound shrimp, peeled
- □ 2 tablespoons (¼ stick) butter, melted
- □ 1 jalapeño pepper, minced
- □ 4 eggs, beaten
- ■ 1 cup heavy cream
- □ Salt, black pepper, and cayenne pepper
- ■ 2 to 3 tablespoons brown sugar

Cut the kernels from the ears of corn. With the back of your knife, scrape the cobs to get all the corn "milk."

If the shrimp are large, cut them in half or into quarters. Mix the corn and shrimp with the butter, jalapeño pepper, eggs, cream, and salt and peppers. Bake in a buttered baking dish (set in a pan of boiling water) at 300 degrees for 30 to 40 minutes, or until the custard is almost set. Sprinkle the top with the brown sugar and run the dish under a hot broiler to brown and form a glaze, watching carefully so the sugar doesn't burn.

⬤ **S**erve with sliced tomatoes and basil. Finish with boysenberry ice and oatmeal cookies.

🍷 **S**omething with a hint of sweetness would take the edge off the hot pepper here: California Chenin Blanc, Orvieto Abboccato, or a Vouvray Demi-Sec.

▶ **M**ake a corn and shrimp soufflé from the same ingredients except the sugar. Scald the cream. Separate 4 eggs. Beat the yolks until foamy; then gradually beat in the cream, corn, shrimp, butter, jalapeño, and seasonings. Beat the egg whites until stiff but not dry and fold into the mixture. Bake in a 6-cup buttered straight-sided baking dish at 375 degrees for 40 to 50 minutes.

BRANDIED CLAM STEW

- ■ 2 dozen hard-shelled clams (the bigger the better)
- ■ ½ cup dry white wine
- □ 4 tablespoons (½ stick) butter
- □ 1 large onion, finely chopped
- □ 1 garlic clove, minced
- ■ 1 Idaho baking potato, peeled and diced
- ■ 1 pint half-and-half
- □ Black pepper, lemon juice, Worcestershire sauce, and Tabasco sauce to taste
- ■ ¼ cup Cognac

Scrub the clams under cold running water to get rid of any sand. Put them into a covered pot with the wine and steam over low heat until the shells open, 10 to 15 minutes. Strain the clam liquid in a strainer lined with cheesecloth or folded paper towels. Remove the clams from their shells and chop the meat.

Melt the butter in your stew pan and sauté the onion and garlic for 3 to 4 minutes. Add the potato, clam broth, and half-and-half. Season, cover the pot, and simmer for 5 minutes. Add the clams and brandy, taste for seasoning, and barely simmer for 5 to 10 minutes, or until the clams and potatoes are tender.

Serve with a cucumber and radish salad.

White Rhône—Hermitage, Crozes-Hermitage, Châteauneuf-du-Pape—makes perfect company for the heartiness of clam stews and chowders. For something a bit lighter, Premier Cru Chablis, Rully, or California Sauvignon Blanc are all possibilities.

Make a clam pie. Prepare the clams and sauté the onion and garlic as above. Cook the remaining ingredients as above, omitting the half-and-half. Add 3 or 4 chopped hard-cooked eggs. Turn into an 8- or 9-inch pie plate. Make an instant piecrust of 1 cup flour, ¼ teaspoon salt, ¼ cup vegetable oil, and 2 tablespoons milk. Use a fork to stir the ingredients together; then roll out the pastry between sheets of plastic wrap. Place the piecrust over the filling in the pie plate, seal the edges, and make a few small slits in the top for steam to escape. Bake at 425 degrees for 12 to 15 minutes.

SOFT-SHELL CRABS IN BLACK BUTTER

■	4	soft-shell crabs
□		Salt, black pepper, and cayenne pepper
□	¼ cup	milk
□	½ cup	flour
□	2 tablespoons	olive oil
□	4 tablespoons (½ stick)	butter
□		Juice of ½ lemon
□	3 tablespoons	chopped parsley
■	1 tablespoon	drained large capers

Cook the crabs as soon as possible after they've been cleaned. Season them well on both sides and pour the milk over them in a dish. Remove the crabs from the milk and dust them with flour.

Heat the oil and half the butter until bubbly in a large skillet. Cook the crabs over medium heat for 3 to 5 minutes a side, or until crisp and golden. Remove to a warm platter. Add the remaining butter and heat until it just begins to brown. Remove the skillet from the heat, add the remaining ingredients, and pour the sauce over the crabs.

◤ Rice is good to soak up the sauce, but so is toast. A radiccio or endive salad makes a nice contrast.

This is an excellent opportunity to go for the best dry white you can afford: Puligny-Montrachet, Meursault, or a full-bodied Chardonnay from one of the top wineries of California or Australia.

For a Chinese flavor, sauté the crabs in peanut oil instead of olive oil; then season the sauce with a teaspoon *each* fermented black beans (available in Oriental stores) and gingerroot, a little minced garlic, a chopped green onion (scallion), dry sherry, and soy sauce or clam juice.

LOBSTER TARRAGON

- 2 lobsters, 1½ pounds each
- 1 cup heavy cream
- ¼ cup Pernod
- 3 tablespoons chopped fresh tarragon, or 1 teaspoon dried
- ☐ Black pepper and cayenne pepper
- ☐ Lemon juice to taste

Bring several quarts of water to boil in a deep pot and add 1 tablespoon of salt for each quart of water. Plunge the lobsters head down into the pot and cover with a lid. Boil for 12 to 15 minutes; then remove the lobsters and run them under cold water until they are cool enough to handle.

Put the lobsters on a cutting board with a well to collect the juices. Cut each lobster in half lengthwise using a sharp knife or kitchen scissors. Cut down the center of the back; then turn the lobster over and repeat on the underside, cutting all the way through the tail meat. Remove the long intestine from the tail, but leave the meat in the shell. Clean the body cavity, discarding the stomach sac, gills, and small legs. Crack claws and remove meat.

Put the green tomalley, the white fat, and any orange coral into a blender. Pour all of the accumulated juices into the blender and add the cream, Pernod, half of the tarragon, and all of the seasonings. Blend until smooth. Pour into a saucepan and bring to a boil. Reduce the sauce until slightly thickened. Pile the claw meat into the cleaned body cavity. Pour the sauce over the tail and claw meat and garnish with the remaining tarragon.

Serve with Yogurt Rice (p. 100) and cassis sorbet.

Lobster is traditionally considered the best partner for the great full-bodied Chardonnays of California or Burgundy, but the Pernod in this version suggests a lighter alternative: Saint-Véran, Pinot Grigio, or an Alsatian Pinot Gris.

For a lobster salad remove all lobster meat from the cooked lobster, cut the tail and claw meat into chunks, and mix with cubes of foie gras pâté and diced raw tomatoes. Put on a bed of arugula or shredded romaine and dress with fresh mayonnaise and lots of tarragon.

Coconut Shellfish Curry

- ☐ 1 small onion, chopped
- ☐ 2 garlic cloves, minced
- ■ 1 jalapeño pepper, minced
- ■ 2 or 3 slices gingerroot, peeled and minced
- ☐ 1 teaspoon paprika
- ☐ 1 tablespoon curry powder
- ☐ Salt, black pepper, and cayenne pepper
- ☐ 2 tablespoons (¼ stick) butter
- ■ 4 plum tomatoes, peeled, seeded, and cubed
- ■ 2 cups fish stock or clam juice
- ■ ¼ cup canned sweetened coconut cream
- ■ 1 to 2 tablespoons lime juice
- ■ 6 small clams in the shell, well scrubbed
- ■ ½ pound shrimp, peeled
- ■ 6 mussels in the shell, well scrubbed
- ☐ 1 tablespoon chopped fresh coriander

In a large skillet with a lid, sauté the onion, garlic, jalapeño pepper, gingerroot, spices, and seasonings in the butter. Add the tomatoes and the stock, mixed with the coconut cream and lime juice. Bring to a boil, add the clams, cover, and simmer for 3 minutes. Add the mussels and shrimp, cover, and steam until all the shells open, 5 to 7 minutes. Serve in soup bowls and sprinkle with coriander.

Serve with plain rice and finish with Avocado-Pineapple Cream (p. 114).

The combination of sweet and sour suggests a wine with an equally ambivalent personality: Alsatian Gewürztraminer or a Riesling from the Rhine or California.

Use the same curried sauce for other fish, such as fillets of flounder, tilefish, red snapper, halibut, or monkfish. Use only ½ cup of stock and simmer the fish in the sauce, covered, until the fish is just cooked through but doesn't fall apart.

OYSTER
CREAM STEW

> ■ 1 pint shucked oysters
> ☐ 1 small onion, minced
> ☐ ¼ teaspoon dried thyme
> ☐ 4 tablespoons (½ stick) butter
> ■ 1 8-ounce bottle clam juice
> ■ 1 pint heavy cream
> ☐ Salt, black pepper, and lemon juice
> ☐ Pinch of grated nutmeg or mace

Drain the oysters over a bowl and save the liquid. Be sure the oysters are free of shell. Sauté the onion and thyme in the butter until tender and scrape into a blender. Add the clam juice and liquefy. Add the oyster liquid, cream, and seasonings and return to the pan. Bring to a simmer and taste for seasoning. (If the liquid has curdled from too-high heat, return it to the blender and liquefy again.) Add the oysters and heat them gently until the edges just begin to curl. Serve in bowls with a grinding of nutmeg on top.

Serve with a Bibb lettuce and cucumber salad. End with a Walnut-Apricot Tart (p. 111).

♀ Muscadet is a traditional partner for oysters, but a somewhat rounder equivalent would be more suitable to the cream: Italian Chardonnay or a Mâcon-Villages would be fine. For more flavor, try an Oregon Chardonnay.

► For a thicker sauce, boil ¼ cup rice with half a minced onion in 1 pint of clam juice until the rice is tender. Add the oyster liquid, mixed with 3 egg yolks and 2 tablespoons lemon juice. Keep the liquid below a simmer and add the oysters. Cook until the edges just begin to curl. Serve garnished with thin lemon slices.

SCALLOPS IN ORANGE BUTTER

- ■ 3 green onions (scallions)
- ■ 1 inch-long piece gingerroot, peeled
- ■ 1 orange
- ☐ 6 tablespoons (¾ stick) butter
- ■ 2 tablespoons dry vermouth
- ■ 1 pound bay scallops (or sea scallops cut in quarters)
- ☐ Salt, black pepper, and cayenne pepper
- ☐ Fresh mint for garnish

Cut the onions into 2-inch lengths and shred them. Shred the gingerroot. Grate the orange rind and set aside. Cut the orange in half and scrape out the pulp.

Melt 2 tablespoons of the butter in a small pan and add the orange pulp, onions, ginger, and vermouth. Barely simmer for 2 or 3 minutes.

Wash the scallops, drain them, and pat them dry with paper towels. Season well with salt and peppers. Melt the remaining butter until bubbly in a large skillet. Add the scallops and shake them in the pan over high heat to barely cook them through, about 1 minute. Turn them into a serving dish and pour the sauce over them. Sprinkle on the orange rind and a few sprigs of fresh mint.

🥣 **S**erve with Zucchini Gratin (p. 105) and end with fresh peaches in champagne.

🍷 **W**hite Châteauneuf-du-Pape or Crozes-Hermitage are good with scallops, or for a more delicate alternative, try a dry California Chenin Blanc or a Vouvray Sec.

▶ **F**or a gratin, put the scallops in a shallow baking dish and cover with a mixture of ½ cup fresh bread crumbs, 2 tablespoons minced parsley (or mint), 1 tablespoon minced garlic, and 2 tablespoons chopped walnuts. Top with ¼ pound (1 stick) butter, cut in slices and strewn over the whole. Bake at 450 degrees on the top rack of the oven for 6 to 10 minutes.

FISH

RED PEPPER SALMON

- ■   2 sweet red peppers
- □   ¼ cup olive oil
- ■   ½ small red onion, chopped
- □   1 garlic clove, minced
- ■   2 anchovy fillets
- □   Black pepper and cayenne pepper
- ■   1 pound salmon steaks or fillets

Roast the peppers under a broiler or directly over a gas flame, turning until the skin is charred on all sides. Put the peppers in a paper bag for 5 minutes to loosen the skin; then peel, seed, and chop the flesh coarsely.

In half the oil, sauté the onion and garlic for 2 or 3 minutes. Put the peppers, onion, garlic, anchovies, and seasonings in a processor or blender and purée. Return to the sauté pan and keep it warm.

Heat the remaining oil in a skillet over high heat and brown the salmon on both sides while keeping the inside pink. Add the pan juices to the sauce, pour the sauce onto a platter, and top with the salmon.

◗ **S**erve with Sesame Eggplant (p. 106) or a red leaf-lettuce salad. End with fresh pears in a chocolate sauce.

Y **A** full-bodied Côtes du Rhône or Gigondas would be substantial enough to negotiate all the flavors here. If you would rather drink a white, try something from the same region, such as Châteauneuf-du-Pape or Crozes-Hermitage. Sauvignon Blanc would be the best choice from California.

► **I**nstead of a red sauce, make a classic green sauce of sorrel (or arugula or watercress). Sauté 1 cup of packed green leaves (stems removed) in 4 tablespoons (½ stick) butter until wilted. Purée in a blender and add ½ cup of crème fraîche or heavy cream. Season with pepper and balsamic vinegar or lemon juice.

SICILIAN SWORDFISH

- ■ 1 pound swordfish (2 1-inch-thick steaks)
- ☐ ¼ cup olive oil
- ☐ 2 garlic cloves, minced
- ■ Fresh thyme, sage, and parsley, chopped
- ☐ Salt, black pepper, and cayenne pepper
- ■ 3 anchovy fillets, mashed
- ☐ ½ lemon
- ■ 1 tablespoon drained capers

Marinate the steaks in a plastic bag in the oil, garlic, half the fresh herbs, and salt and peppers, for as long as you can (30 minutes to 6 hours).

Brown the fish on both sides in a hot skillet (add more oil if needed), lower the heat slightly, and cook until the flesh inside turns from translucent to opaque, 5 to 8 minutes. *Don't* overcook or the fish will be tough and dry. Put the steaks on a warm plate.

Stir the mashed anchovies into the pan juices and squeeze in the lemon juice. Add the capers and the remaining fresh herbs. Swirl and pour the sauce over the fish.

● **G**ood with a Roasted Pepper Salad (p. 2) and a plain shell pasta.

Y **A** good California Chardonnay will match the richness of the dish. For an interesting alternative, try a Chardonnay or Sauvignon Blanc from Australia.

► **B**roil or bake a swordfish steak by coating it in oil and then a mixture of garlic and fresh or dried herbs, such as rosemary and thyme. Broil close to the heat source for 3 to 5 minutes on each side or in a 450-degree oven for 10 minutes. Serve with a garnish of Mediterranean black olives chopped together with garlic and lemon rind.

Asparagus Bass

- ■   1   pound striped bass, tilefish, whitefish, etc. fillets
- ☐   Salt, black pepper, and cayenne pepper
- ☐   2   tablespoons lemon juice
- ☐   4   tablespoons (½ stick) butter
- ■   1   pound asparagus
- ■   2   tablespoons sour cream

Season the fish and sprinkle it with lemon juice; then dot with 2 tablespoons of the butter and bake in a buttered pan at 350 degrees for 5 to 10 minutes.

Meanwhile, wash the asparagus and break off the tough ends. Peel the stems and then chop them to an inch below the tips. Reserve the tips and put the stems in a pan and add salted water to cover. Boil until the stems are very tender. Remove with a slotted spoon to a blender. Put the asparagus tips in the same water and simmer until just tender, 3 to 4 minutes. Remove to a warm dish.

Pour off all but 1 cup of the asparagus water and boil down to 2 tablespoons. Add to the blender. Add the pan juices of the baked fish along with the sour cream to the blender and purée until smooth. Arrange the fish on a warm platter, pour on the sauce, and arrange the asparagus tips on top.

🍲 Serve with boiled new potatoes or Garlic Roast Potatoes (p. 102). End with bananas sautéed in butter, molasses, and rum.

🍷 The special taste of asparagus is best complemented by Sauvignon Blanc from California or Italy, or its equivalent in a white Graves, Sancerre, or Pouilly Fumé.

▶ Make a different kind of green sauce with spinach and watercress or arugula. Wilt 2 cups of packed leaves in 2 tablespoons (¼ stick) of butter. Purée in a blender with 1 cup of yogurt. Add lemon juice to taste.

Skillet-
Smoked Tuna

- ■ 1 pound tuna (1½-inches thick)
- ■ 1 tablespoon peanut oil
- ☐ 3 tablespoons crushed coriander seeds
- ☐ 1 teaspoon cumin seeds
- ☐ ¼ cup black tea leaves
- ■ ¼ cup brown rice
- ■ ¼ cup brown sugar
- ■ ¼ cup fresh coriander leaves, chopped
- ■ 3 or 4 slices gingerroot, peeled and minced
- ☐ 2 tablespoons (¼ stick) butter, softened
- ☐ Lemon juice to taste

In a very hot wok or heavy skillet, heat the peanut oil, sear the tuna quickly on both sides, and remove. Wipe out the pan and line it with aluminum foil. Spread it with a mixture of the seeds, tea, rice, and sugar. Line a wok cover or skillet lid with foil. Place a rack, large enough to hold the fish, inside the wok or skillet on top of the spices. Cover and heat over high heat for 5 minutes. Place the tuna on the rack and cover again. Turn the heat to low and smoke the fish for 10 minutes. Remove from the heat and let sit for 10 minutes with the lid on.

Mix the coriander and ginger with the butter and lemon juice. Garnish the smoked fish with the butter.

🥣 Serve with Pears in Chinese Hot Sauce (p. 107).

🍷 Try a white Graves or a full-bodied California Sauvignon Blanc to complement the smoked flavor, or else a fairly dry Riesling from California or the Rhine for an interesting alternative.

▶ Marinate tuna or other fish fillets (mackerel, shad, eel, or small whole fish, such as snapper or trout), in a fresh coriander sauce of ¼ cup coriander, 1 garlic clove, 2 slices gingerroot, a pinch of cumin seeds and cayenne pepper, a dash of lemon juice, and ¼ cup oil for 40 minutes. Smoke as above without browning the fish first, or broil the fish without smoking.

CARAMELIZED ONION COD

■	3	large onions
☐	2	tablespoons olive oil
☐	2	tablespoons (¼ stick) butter
☐	¼	teaspoon ground turmeric
☐	1¼	teaspoon ground ginger
■	1	pound cod (2 1½-inch-thick steaks)
☐		Salt and black pepper

In a heavy skillet, sauté the onions, turmeric, and ginger over low heat in the oil and butter until caramel colored, about 30 to 40 minutes. Season the cod with the salt and pepper and let sit while the onions are cooking.

Put a layer of the onions in a baking dish, put the cod on top, and cover with another layer of onions. Cover the dish with a tight lid or aluminum foil, sealing the edges. Bake at 400 degrees for 8 to 12 minutes.

Serve with Yogurt Rice (p. 100) and steamed baby carrots.

♈ **A** moderately priced Chardonnay from California or Italy would be most suitable, or else a white Rully or Mâcon-Villages.

▶ **B**ake cod or other white fish (halibut, haddock, or tilefish) in a cup of heavy cream with a cup of minced onions, some minced garlic, and fresh basil or mint. To thicken the sauce, purée the cream, onion, garlic, and pan juices in a blender. Add a smoked mussel to the blender for a darker flavor.

BIRDS

AVOCADO-LIME CHICKEN

- ■ 2 boned chicken breasts
- □ Salt, black pepper, and cayenne pepper
- ■ ¾ cup heavy cream
- □ ¼ teaspoon ground cumin
- □ ½ teaspoon ground coriander
- ■ ½ ripe avocado, peeled and cubed
- ■ Rind and juice of 2 limes

Skin the breasts, flatten them slightly (a rolling pin or a heavy jar will do it), and slice them lengthwise into ½-inch-wide strips. Season them well with the salt and peppers. In a skillet, bring the cream to a boil with the cumin and coriander, add the chicken, and barely simmer 1 to 2 minutes a side. Remove the chicken slices to a warm plate. Boil the cream to thicken it, add the avocado cubes, and lime juice to taste. Pour the sauce over the chicken and sprinkle with the grated rind.

This super-quick dish is good cold or hot. It goes well with a tomato vinaigrette.

♥ **A** dry white with good acidity will help to balance the avocado: Sancerre, Pouilly Fumé, white Graves, or Sauvignon Blanc from California. New York Chardonnay is another possibility.

► **M**ake chicken slices in a pâte-cream sauce. Purée in a blender ½ cup heavy cream, ¼ cup chicken stock, 2 tablespoons pâté fois gras (or 2 chicken livers cut in pieces and sautéed lightly in butter), ½ teaspoon balsamic vinegar, and lemon juice to taste. Pour the sauce in a skillet and simmer as above. If you like, garnish the slices with cubes of fois gras.

TURKISH WALNUT CHICKEN

- ■ 2 boned chicken breasts
- ■ 2 tablespoons walnut oil
- ☐ Black pepper and cayenne pepper
- ☐ 1 small onion, finely chopped
- ■ ½ cup dry white wine
- ☐ 1 tablespoon lemon juice
- ■ 1 cup walnuts
- ☐ Paprika

Coat the chicken breasts with half the walnut oil and season them well on both sides with the peppers. In a large skillet, sauté the onion in the remaining oil until transparent. Add the wine and chicken, cover tightly, and simmer over very low heat for 6 to 10 minutes, turning the chicken once. Cut into the breast at its thickest part to test for doneness. The chicken should just lose its translucence—don't overcook.

Pour the pan juices into a blender, add the lemon juice and walnuts, and purée. Thin if necessary with a little more wine, or with yogurt or cream. Spread the sauce over the breasts and sprinkle with paprika.

■ Serve with Sesame Eggplant (p. 106) and finish with a fresh fruit salad sprinkled with cumin seeds.

▼ Two directions are possible here: either Italian, Oregon or New York Chardonnay to go with the lemon and white wine, or a light red Burgundy, such as Mercurey or Côte de Beaune-Villages to bring out the flavor of the walnuts.

► For deep-fried walnut chicken, cut the breasts in chunks and season. Dip them in a batter of 2 egg whites beaten with 1½ tablespoons cornstarch or arrowroot. Roll them in 1 cup ground nuts, pressing the nuts in all around. Refrigerate for 30 minutes. Heat 2 cups of peanut or other vegetable oil in a wok or heavy skillet until hot but not smoking (350 degrees) and fry the chicken chunks quickly, two or three at a time. Drain on paper towels.

PEANUT CHICKEN LEGS

- ■ 2 chicken legs with thighs attached
- ■ 2 tablespoons peanut oil
- ☐ 1 clove garlic, mashed
- ☐ 1 tablespoon soy sauce
- ■ 3 or 4 slices gingerroot, peeled and minced
- ☐ 1 tablespoon wine vinegar
- ☐ Hot red pepper flakes or cayenne pepper
- ■ ¼ cup dry sherry, vermouth, or chicken stock
- ■ 2 tablespoons fresh crunchy peanut butter
- ☐ 1 tablespoon salted peanuts for garnish

Brown the legs on both sides in the peanut oil over high heat. Add the remaining ingredients, except the peanut butter and peanuts. Cover the skillet, lower the heat, and cook chicken until tender, 25 to 30 minutes. Turn the chicken at least once. Remove the chicken to a warm serving platter.

Stir the peanut butter into the pan juices. Thin with sherry if the sauce is too thick. Pour the sauce over the chicken and sprinkle with peanuts. Serve hot, at room temperature, or cold.

▬ **G**ood with a crisp salad of Jerusalem artichokes or string beans.

▯ **T**ry a chilled bottle of Beaujolais-Villages (preferably from a top producer like Duboeuf) or, for a white, California Riesling.

▬ **B**aked parmesan chicken legs. Dip the legs in ¼ cup melted butter seasoned with Worcestershire sauce and Dijon mustard. Roll the legs in 1 cup fresh bread crumbs mixed with ¼ cup *each* grated Parmesan cheese and minced parsley. Season with salt and pepper and bake at 350 degrees for 50 to 60 minutes.

TURKEY TONNATO

- ■ 1 pound turkey cutlets (¼-inch-thick breast slices)
- □ 2 tablespoons olive oil
- ■ ¼ cup dry white wine
- ■ ¼ cup canned tuna, drained
- ■ 2 anchovy fillets
- □ 2 tablespoons lemon juice
- □ 2 tablespoons mayonnaise
- ■ ½ cup yogurt
- □ Black pepper
- ■ 2 tablespoons large capers, drained

Sauté the turkey slices quickly on both sides in the olive oil, about 1 minute on each side. Put on a serving platter. Pour the pan juices into a blender with all the remaining ingredients, except the capers. Purée to make the tuna-cream sauce (*tonnato,* as the Italians say) and pour the sauce over the slices. Sprinkle with the capers.

Serve with an Italian flat bread like foccacia and a fava bean salad.

Ⴎ **A** Mâcon-Villages would suit well here, or a white Rully for more flavor. Other possibilities include Chardonnays from Italy, Oregon, or New York.

► **T**he same sauce is traditional with cold veal slices, but if you like the combination of tuna and turkey, a nifty cold dish is made by piling turkey slices (sautéed as above or leftover from a roast or cut from a smoked turkey) with tuna tartare. Buy ¼ pound fresh tuna. Chop it coarsely with a little onion, garlic, anchovy, and parsley. Season it with lemon juice and pepper, brandy if wanted, and sprinkle it with capers.

Marmalade Duck

- ■ 1 4- to 5-pound fresh duck, cut into pieces
- □ Salt, black pepper, and cayenne pepper
- ■ ½ cup bitter orange marmalade
- □ 2 tablespoons lemon juice
- □ 1 tablespoon Dijon mustard
- □ 1 navel orange, thinly sliced

Remove all the excess fat from the duck that you can. Prick the skin of the breasts and thighs with a fork all over to release the fat when cooking. Season well with the salt and peppers.

Mix the marmalade with the lemon and mustard. Coat the breast and thighs with the marmalade mixture and place on a rack in a roasting pan. Roast at 375 degrees for 15 minutes. Remove the breast. Prick the skin of the thighs again and let them continue to roast another 15 minutes.

Put the breasts and thighs skin-side up on aluminum foil or a broiler pan, heat the broiler and broil the meat for 5 to 10 minutes to crisp the skin and complete the cooking. Put the orange slices over the top.

Serve with Fresh Potato Chips (p. 4) and end with dried figs and walnuts.

Something on the sweeter side will complement the marmalade, such as California Riesling, Mosel Spätlese, or Gewürztraminer from Alsace. For a suitable red, try a Mercurey, Santenay, or Chassagne-Montrachet from Burgundy.

Do a duck sauté. Prick the skin thoroughly. Sauté the meat in a hot skillet, skin side down. Remove the breasts after 5 minutes. Turn the thighs and brown on the other side. Pour off the fat. Add ½ cup good barbecue sauce thinned with white wine and ½ cup Mediterranean green olives. Simmer the thighs until tender, covered. Add the breasts just before serving.

GIN QUAIL

■	2	fresh quail
☐		Salt, black pepper, and cayenne pepper
☐		Flour
☐	2	tablespoons (¼ stick) butter
☐	2	tablespoons olive oil
☐	2 or 3	bay leaves, crushed
■	6	juniper berries, crushed
■	¼	cup gin
■	½	cup dry white wine

Split each quail with a knife or poultry shears along the back and flatten it with your hands. Season the birds well and dust them with flour. Heat the butter and oil with the bay and juniper. Brown the quail on both sides; then lower the heat and sauté until tender, 3 to 4 minutes. Warm the gin, pour it over the birds and flame them with a match. Remove the birds to a serving platter. Add the wine to the pan juices, reduce rapidly, and pour over the birds.

Serve with toast points or Nutted Wild Rice (p. 101) and young dandelion or other sharp greens.

Y This calls for a wine with plenty of flavor that isn't too heavy on the palate: Mercurey, Santenay, or a Savigny from Burgundy, Vacqueyras from the Rhone, or a red Rioja from Spain. If you like a more full-bodied red, look for an Oregon Pinot Noir or a young St. Emilion.

► Roast the quail whole by stuffing each with 2 or 3 oysters, 3 tablespoons butter, and chopped parsley. Season the outside with salt and pepper, wrap each bird in 2 or 3 strips of bacon, and put breast up in a roasting pan. Roast at 450 degrees for 10 minutes, or until the bacon is crisp. Remove the bacon and brown the birds another 5 minutes. Crumble the bacon over the top for serving.

MEAT

VEAL CHOPS IN BRANDY CREAM

- ■ ½ ounce dried porcini mushrooms
- ■ 1 cup heavy cream
- ■ ⅛ pound prosciutto
- ■ 2 veal chops (1-inch thick)
- ☐ Salt and black pepper
- ☐ 2 tablespoons (¼ stick) butter
- ☐ 2 tablespoons olive oil
- ■ ¼ cup Cognac

Pour 1 cup of boiling water over the mushrooms and soak for 30 minutes. Strain and save the soaking liquid. Rinse the mushrooms, drain, and chop fine. Put the mushrooms in a bowl and add the cream. Strain the mushroom liquid through a doubled paper towel and add to the cream. Shred the prosciutto and add half of it to the cream.

Season the chops with salt and pepper and brown them in a skillet in the hot oil and butter, about 3 minutes on each side. Add the mushroom cream, cover the skillet, and simmer for 10 to 15 minutes. Remove the chops to a warm platter. Add the Cognac to the sauce and reduce it quickly until the sauce has thickened slightly. Pour the sauce over the chops and sprinkle with the remaining prosciutto.

erve with a salad of arugula and diced tomatoes.

his deserves the best bottle of full-bodied dry white wine you can come up with to match the richness of the mushrooms and the sauce: Meursault or a close equivalent from Burgundy, or else a big Chardonnay from California or Australia.

or simple herbed chops, season the chops, dust them lightly with flour, and press into both sides a mixture of chopped fresh herbs, such as sage, rosemary, and thyme. Brown the chops quickly in the hot butter and oil. Add ¼ cup dry white wine or vermouth, cover, and simmer for 10 minutes or so.

LEMON VEAL SCALLOPS

■	1	pound veal scallops
☐	2	lemons
■	1	cup fresh bread crumbs
■	½	cup grated Parmesan cheese
☐		Salt and black pepper
☐	1	egg
☐	4	tablespoons (½ stick) butter
☐	2	tablespoons olive oil
☐	1	tablespoon chopped parsley

If the scallops are not ⅛ inch thick, pound them until they are (a rolling pin or heavy jar will do it).

Grate the rind of 1 lemon and mix with the crumbs, cheese, and seasonings. Beat the egg with 2 tablespoons of lemon juice. Dip each scallop in the egg and then in the crumb mixture.

Heat the butter and oil in a large skillet until bubbly. Add the scallops, two or three at a time, and sauté as quickly as possible, about ½ minute on each side. Transfer to a warm platter and keep warm. Add more butter or oil, if needed, until all the scallops are browned.

Add another tablespoon of lemon juice to the pan juices and pour over the scallops. Slice 1 lemon and put the slices over the scallops. Sprinkle with the parsley.

◖ Serve with a butter and cheese pasta and an asparagus vinaigrette.

🍷 The combination of lemon and veal suggests a white with a fair amount of acidity: Sancerre, Premier Cru Chablis, or white Graves. A white Mercurey or Auxey-Duresses from Burgundy would present a softer alternative. For something less expensive, look for a Mâcon-Villages or Italian Chardonnay.

► For traditional veal scalloppine, instead of breading the scallops, dust them with seasoned flour and sauté. Add ½ cup heavy cream and ¼ cup Marsala, Madeira, or dry sherry to the pan juices and pour the sauce over the scallops.

ARTICHOKED LAMB

- ■ 2 loin lamb chops (1½-inches thick)
- ☐ 2 tablespoons olive oil
- ■ 4 canned artichoke hearts, quartered
- ■ 2 Belgian endive, halved
- ☐ 6 garlic cloves, halved
- ■ 12 Mediterranean olives, green or black
- ☐ 1 teaspoon mixed dried herbs, such as sage, rosemary, thyme, and oregano
- ☐ Salt and black pepper

Heat the olive oil in a skillet over high heat and sear the lamb chops quickly on both sides. Arrange the chops with the vegetables, garlic, and olives in a baking dish, sprinkle them with the herbs and seasonings, and pour the pan juices over the whole. Cover the dish with aluminum foil and seal the edges tightly. Bake at 325 degrees for 15 or 20 minutes for rare to medium-rare lamb.

Serve with crusty French bread to absorb the garlic and juices. End with Margarita Oranges (p. 110).

Lamb is the traditional match for a good red Bordeaux from the Médoc. The artichokes, however, change things slightly, suggesting the less austere qualities of a Pomerol or a good California Merlot. If you like a strong red, try a northern Rhône, such as Cornas or Saint Joseph, or wines made elsewhere from the same grape: California Syrah or Australian Shiraz.

To make a Lamb Ratatouille, sear the chops as above, but instead of endive and artichoke hearts, add cubed eggplant, zucchini, fresh tomatoes, and minced onion to the skillet with the garlic and herbs. Cover and cook over low heat for 10 to 15 minutes.

Braised Sweetbreads

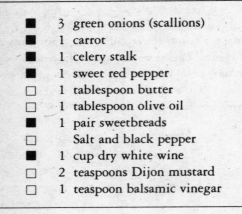

- ■ 3 green onions (scallions)
- ■ 1 carrot
- ■ 1 celery stalk
- ■ 1 sweet red pepper
- □ 1 tablespoon butter
- □ 1 tablespoon olive oil
- ■ 1 pair sweetbreads
- □ Salt and black pepper
- ■ 1 cup dry white wine
- □ 2 teaspoons Dijon mustard
- □ 1 teaspoon balsamic vinegar

Finely chop all the vegetables and then sauté them until lightly browned in the butter and oil. Lay the sweetbreads on top, season well, and pour in the wine. Cook, covered, over low heat for 30 minutes. Remove the sweetbreads to a plate, put a board or a plate on top and weight with a can to press the sweetbreads slightly.

Purée the vegetables in a processor or blender. If the sweetbreads have not been trimmed, remove the outside membranes and connecting tubes. Add the trimmings to the processor. Add the mustard and vinegar and process again. Taste for seasoning. Cut the sweetbreads crosswise in 1 inch-thick slices. Reheat briefly in the skillet with the puréed sauce.

◗ Serve with a crisp green salad and baked chèvre (herbed and oiled, and baked at 350 degrees for 10 minutes.)

🍷 The delicacy of the sweetbreads suggests either a medium-bodied red Bordeaux from Margaux or St. Julien or a similar red Burgundy (try Fixin or Savigny). Red Rioja is another attractive possibility.

▶ For broiled sweetbreads: if the sweetbreads are not trimmed, parboil them gently in simmering water with a little salt and lemon juice for 15 minutes. Drain and run under cold water. Trim off the membranes and tubes and discard. Spread the sweetbreads with Dijon mustard and roll them in bread crumbs mixed with chopped fresh herbs. Broil or sauté until the crumbs are well browned on all sides.

NORMANDY PORK SCALLOPS

> ■ 1 pound pork scallops
> □ Salt and black pepper
> □ Flour
> □ 1 tablespoon olive oil
> □ 4 tablespoons (½ stick) butter
> ■ 2 tart green apples
> □ 1 small onion, sliced
> ■ 2 tablespoons Calvados

Pound the scallops, if needed, to make them ¼-inch thick. Season, dredge with the flour, and brown quickly on both sides (1 to 2 minutes on each side) in a skillet in the oil and butter. Remove the pork and set aside.

Quarter the apples, core and peel them, and slice them ½-inch thick. Sauté the onion and apples in the hot butter until they are lightly browned. Add the Calvados and the pork, cover the skillet, and simmer for 3 to 4 minutes, or until the pork is just cooked through but not dried out.

◗ Pork is always good with noodles or potatoes. End with a plum tart.

Y **R**ed and white are equally good here. The apples will be best matched by a California Riesling or Mosel Kabinett. For a red, try Merlot or Cabernet from Long Island, Italian Merlot, or else a Chinon or Bourgueil from the Loire.

► **D**o a Chinese pork stir-fry. Brown the pork scallops quickly in 2 tablespoons of peanut oil. Add minced hot pepper, gingerroot, garlic, and green onions (scallions), and fry for 1 minute. Add 1 tablespoon soy sauce, 2 tablespoons dry sherry, and 1 teaspoon wine vinegar. Cook for 1 minute and transfer to a platter. Sprinkle the pork with toasted sesame seeds.

BEEF FILET PROVENÇALE

- ■ 1 pound trimmed beef filet
- □ 1 small onion, finely chopped
- □ 1 garlic clove, minced
- ■ ¼ cup chopped fresh Italian parsley
- □ 1 bay leaf, crushed
- □ Salt and black pepper
- ■ ½ cup red wine
- ■ 1 tablespoon Cognac
- □ 2 tablespoons olive oil
- ■ 2 to 3 wild mushrooms
- ■ ¼ cup black Mediterranean olives, pitted and chopped

Marinate the filet in a mixture of the onion, garlic, parsley, bay leaf, seasonings, wine, and Cognac for 30 minutes (or longer, if you can), turning the meat at least once. Remove the filet from the marinade and pat it dry. Put it in a roasting pan, baste it with half the olive oil, and roast at 500 degrees for 20 minutes, turning the meat after 10 minutes so it roasts evenly. The interior of the meat is done when a meat thermometer registers 120 degrees. Let the meat rest for 10 minutes before slicing it into ½-inch-thick slices.

While the meat is resting, slice the mushrooms thickly and sauté them in the remaining oil over high heat to brown them quickly. Remove the mushrooms from the pan and set aside. To the same pan, add the olives, the marinade, and the juices from the roasting pan and boil for 2 to 3 minutes. For a richer sauce, beat in 2 tablespoons of butter, off the heat. Pour the sauce over the sliced beef and strew the mushrooms over the top.

◗ Serve with a plain potato pancake and a mixed vegetable salad. End with a Frozen Chocolate Truffle (p. 115).

🍷 Bandol would serve as a good traditional match from Provence, but you might also take the opportunity to enjoy a good California Cabernet, its equivalent from Australia or Spain, or one of the sturdier red Bordeaux from Pauillac or St. Estèphe.

► For filet mignon, saute 2 thick filet steaks over high heat in butter and oil to make them crusty on the outside but rare inside for about 2 to 3 minutes on each side. Remove the steaks and sauté the chopped garlic and wild mushrooms in the same pan. Loosen the pan juices with a splash of Madeira or Cognac and pour the contents of the pan over the steaks.

Rabbit Mole

■	1	2- to 3-pound fresh rabbit, cut into pieces
□		Flour, salt, and black pepper
□	¼	cup olive oil
□	1	small onion, chopped
□	2	garlic cloves, mashed
■	¼	cup pumpkin seeds
■	2	tablespoons sunflower seeds
□	¼	teaspoon cumin seeds
□	1	dried red chili pepper
■	3	sprigs fresh coriander
■	1	cup chicken broth
■	1	tablespoon grated bitter chocolate

Dust the rabbit pieces with seasoned flour. Heat the oil in a heavy skillet and brown the pieces on both sides. Remove the rabbit and in the same pan sauté the onion, garlic, seeds, and crumbled chili pepper for 5 minutes. Put in a blender with the coriander, broth, and chocolate and purée. Taste for seasoning and adjust, making it hotter with more chili or blander with more pumpkin seeds. Return the rabbit to the pan, pour the sauce over it, cover, and simmer for 20 to 30 minutes.

Serve with a salad of arugula and oranges. End with guava paste and mascarpone served on crisp crackers.

Certain red wines have a "chocolaty" quality that goes well with mole: try a medium-bodied Zinfandel, a Nebbiolo d'Alba, or a sturdy Rhône red like Gigondas.

Stuff a whole rabbit with fresh bread crumbs mixed with chopped and sautéed mushrooms, garlic, and the rabbit liver if available. Season well. Coat the rabbit with oil and roast at 400 degrees for 50 to 60 minutes. Melt 4 tablespoons (½ stick) butter and baste the rabbit while it is roasting. When the rabbit is done, sauté ¼ pound wild mushrooms and 1 clove minced garlic in the basting butter and use as a sauce.

VENISON STEAKS

■	1	pound venison steaks (1½ inches thick)
☐		Salt and coarsely ground black pepper
☐	2	tablespoons (¼ stick) butter
☐	2	tablespoons olive oil
☐	½	small hot pepper, minced
■	1	tablespoon tomato paste
■	1	tablespoon cranberry preserves or currant jelly
☐	1	tablespoon red wine vinegar
■	2	tablespoons port or Madeira
■	½	cup red wine
☐		Dash of Worcestershire sauce

Season the steaks well on both sides. Heat the butter and oil in a heavy skillet and sear the steaks on both sides, 5 to 7 minutes a side for rare meat. Transfer the steaks to a hot platter and make the game sauce by stirring the remaining ingredients into the pan juices. Bring to a boil, taste for sweet and sour, and adjust by adding more cranberry preserves or vinegar. Pour the sauce over the steaks.

◗ Serve with a good winter vegetable, such as puréed turnips, and end with Maple Toffee Apples or Pears (p. 113).

🍷 The richness of game calls for the strongest reds of all: full-bodied Cabernets or Zinfandels from California (Ridge Vineyards is an excellent source for both varieties), a Hermitage, Côte Rôtie, or good Châteauneuf-du-Pape from the Rhône, or a good Barolo or Barbaresco from Italy. Red Bordeaux from the northern Médoc (Pauillac or St. Estèphe) would also make an excellent match.

▶ For broiled steaks, season the steaks and coat them with oil. Broil close to the flame, 4 minutes on each side. Top each steak with a large spoonful of herb butter (mix 4 tablespoons (½ stick) softened butter with chopped parsley and garlic, or chopped basil, thyme, rosemary, mint, oregano—whatever you can get fresh).

Misc.

TRUFFLED EGGS

■	2	fresh black truffles
■	6	eggs
☐		Salt and black pepper
☐	6	tablespoons (¾ stick) butter

Clean the truffles by scrubbing them with a vegetable brush under cold running water; then dice them fine.

Beat the eggs with the salt and pepper, and stir in the truffles (if you have any time before eating, put the mixture in an airtight container to get maximum truffle symbiosis).

Melt the butter in a non-stick or well-seasoned skillet. Add the eggs and cook gently over very low heat, stirring constantly with a spatula or wooden spoon to cook the eggs evenly. While the eggs are still soft and almost runny, scoop them onto warm plates.

Serve with toasted pita halves, English muffins, or croissants. Follow with a green salad, ripe pears, and chèvre.

🍷 **T**ry a sparkling Rosé to play off the earthiness of the truffles: Bouvet is a good choice from the Loire or, for a special treat, look for Charbaut.

► **M**ake a Truffled Omelet. For each person, use ½ truffle and 2 tablespoons diced foie gras pâté to 3 eggs. Cook one omelet at a time. Mix the diced truffles and pâté together. Heat 1½ tablespoons of butter until it is bubbling, and add the beaten eggs. With the back of a fork, push the edges of the cooked eggs toward the middle of the pan. Top each omelet with half the truffle mixture. Fold the omelet over as you slide it onto a plate. For detailed instructions, see Crab and Avocado Omelet (p. 84).

CRAB AND AVOCADO OMELET

- [ ] 4 tablespoons (½ stick) butter
- [x] 1 cup lump crab meat, well drained
- [x] 1 ripe avocado, peeled and diced
- [ ] 1 tablespoon lemon juice
- [ ] ½ teaspoon ground cumin
- [ ] Salt, black pepper, and cayenne pepper
- [x] 1 cup sour cream
- [ ] 6 eggs

Melt 2 tablespoons of the butter. Add the crab, avocado, lemon juice, cumin, and other seasonings to taste, and heat gently over low heat. Remove from the heat and mix with the sour cream.

Make one omelet at a time in a non-stick skillet (8 to 9 inches is best). Beat the eggs with a fork and season with the salt and peppers. In the skillet, heat 1 tablespoon of the remaining butter over fairly high heat until the butter bubbles and just begins to brown. Add half the eggs, give them 2 seconds to form a film on the bottom of the pan; then, with the back of a fork, push the edges of the cooked eggs toward the middle of the pan to let the unset egg on top contact the hot metal on the bottom (less than a minute).

Spoon half the filling on top of the eggs. Tip the pan away from you over a warm plate and roll the omelet over on itself as you tip it onto the plate. (There's a lot of filling in this omelet and a lot will run out. Don't worry.) Repeat with the remaining butter, eggs and filling.

Serve with buttered Melba toast and toasted French bread, a leaf-lettuce salad, and fresh figs with triple cream cheese.

Dry Chenin blanc from California or its counterpart, a Vouvray Sec from the Loire, would be best. For brunch, a sparkling Vouvray or Saumur might be even better.

Make a well-seasoned salad of the crab and avocado on a bed of shredded salad greens, surrounded by quartered hard-cooked eggs and green olives. Serve with a mayonnaise spiked with lime juice, mustard, and sherry vinegar or brandy.

Ricotta Greens

■ 1 pound mixed greens (dandelion, mustard, turnip, curly endive, or watercress)
☐ 1 small onion, minced
☐ 1 garlic clove, minced
☐ 2 tablespoons olive oil
■ 1 cup ricotta cheese
■ ½ cup grated Parmesan cheese
■ ½ cup heavy cream
☐ 2 eggs, beaten
☐ 1 to 2 tablespoons lemon juice
■ 4 sprigs fresh mint or basil
☐ Salt, black pepper, and cayenne pepper

Cut off and discard the stems; then wash the greens well.

In a big skillet with a lid, sauté the onion and garlic in the oil briefly. Add the greens, cover, and cook over low heat until the greens are tender, 10 to 20 minutes, depending on the greens. Drain, chop coarsely, drain again, and save juice for another purpose, like soup.

Purée the remaining ingredients in a blender or processor and mix with the greens in a buttered baking dish. Cover with a lid or aluminum foil and bake at 325 degrees for 20 to 30 minutes, or until the eggs are set.

Serve with smoked capon, smoked fish, or delicatessen meats like prosciutto.

A fairly tart white is required to play off the bitterness of the greens. Try Sancerre or Pouilly Fumé from the Loire, Premier Cru Chablis, white Graves, or a California Sauvignon Blanc.

Serve the same greens as a salad with a hot dressing. Cut 2 or 3 thick slices of smoked bacon into strips and fry until crisp. Sprinkle them over the chopped raw greens. Add 2 teaspoons wine vinegar to 2 tablespoons hot fat and pour over the greens.

Bacon and Potato Pancake

- ■ 8 slices bacon (or 1 cup pork, duck, or chicken cracklings)
- ■ 2 large Idaho potatoes
- ☐ 4 tablespoons bacon or beef fat
- ■ 2 green onions (scallions), chopped
- ■ ¼ cup minced parsley
- ☐ ¼ teaspoon dried thyme
- ☐ Salt and black pepper

Snip the bacon crosswise into ¼-inch strips and fry in a large skillet. Remove the bacon to paper towels with a slotted spoon and pour off all but 4 tablespoons of fat.

Scrub the potatoes and grate them, skin and all, in a processor or by hand. Heat the fat in the skillet over high heat and spread the potatoes to cover the bottom of the pan. Sprinkle the potatoes with onions, bacon, parsley, and seasonings. Flatten the pancake with a spatula to mix in the garnishes and get a good crust. Turn the heat to medium.

When the bottom of the pancake is well browned, slide it onto a large plate, invert the skillet over the plate and turn right side up so that the uncooked side of the pancake is on the bottom of the skillet. Brown the bottom of the pancake for 5 to 8 minutes, and slip it onto a serving plate. Cut in quarters to serve.

◗ Serve with Broccoli and Cauliflowerets (p. 104) and follow with ripe melon sprinkled with salt and lime.

𝚼 Try a useful dry white, like a Mâcon-Villages or a dry Orvieto, or California Pinot Blanc. If you prefer red, a Beaujolais-Villages would be fine.

▶ Make a pastrami hash. Dice ¼ pound pastrami (or corned beef) and add to the grated potatoes, onions, and parsley. Add a mashed anchovy for salt. Fry in beef or chicken fat, if possible.

Eggplant
Torta

- ■ ½ pound eggplant
- ☐ 1 large onion
- ■ 2 ripe tomatoes
- ☐ Salt, black pepper, and dried oregano
- ☐ ¼ cup olive oil
- ■ ¾ cup ricotta cheese
- ☐ 1 garlic clove, minced
- ■ ¼ cup fresh Italian parsley, chopped
- ■ ⅛ pound mozzarella, sliced
- ■ ¼ cup grated Parmesan cheese

Slice the eggplant into ¼-inch-thick slices and place on top of aluminum foil on a broiling rack. Slice the onion the same thickness. Cut the tomatoes in half and squeeze out the seeds. Put the onion and tomatoes, cut side up, on the same broiling rack. Season the vegetables with salt, pepper, and oregano and dribble the oil over the top. Broil for 3 to 5 minutes, or until the tops are browned.

Mix the ricotta with the garlic and parsley. In a baking dish, place half the eggplant, browned side up, in a single layer on the bottom, and top with half the onion slices and tomatoes. (Press the tomatoes flat with a fork.) Cover with the ricotta and half the mozzarella. Layer the remaining tomatoes, onions, and eggplant, browned side down, and top with the remaining mozzarella and Parmesan. Bake at 350 degrees for 25 to 35 minutes.

■ Serve with shrimp and Tapenade Dip (p. 5) to start, and end with sweet red seedless grapes.

♟ A good medium-bodied Zinfandel, such as Sutter Home, will do well here, or a Chianti Classico. For something slightly different, a Bandol (look for Domaine Tempier) from Provence would be an excellent choice.

► Make a ratatouille by frying the onion, garlic, cubed eggplant, sweet red and green peppers, zucchini, and tomatoes in olive oil and chopped herbs. Add a crumbled poached Italian sausage, such as cotechino, or cubed fried sweet or hot Italian sausages, together with pitted black olives.

GREEN CHILI SOUP

- ■ 1 4-ounce can green chilis (non-pickled)
- ■ 2 small zucchini or 1 pattypan squash
- ■ 3 ears corn
- ■ 3 cups chicken stock
- ☐ 2 tablespoons (¼ stick) butter
- ☐ Salt and black pepper
- ■ ¼ cup sour cream
- ☐ Garnish: avocado or fresh coriander

Dice the chilis (for a milder chili, remove the seeds and veins before dicing). Dice the squash. Remove the corn kernels from the cobs by standing each cob on end and slicing down. Then, with the back of your knife, scrape the cob to get all the corn "milk."

Put half the chilis and half the corn into a blender and purée. Bring the stock to a boil in a large saucepan and add the purée and zucchini. Simmer for 2 to 3 minutes, or until the squash is almost tender. Add the butter, remaining chilis, corn, and seasonings and simmer for 1 minute. Pour into bowls and top with a dollop of sour cream and diced avocado or chopped coriander.

■ **S**erve with hot buttered tortillas. Follow with Sliced mangoes or papaya.

🍷 **A** cold rosé with a little sweetness to it will most effectively quench the fire of the chili. Try Rosé d'Anjou, Zinfandel Rosé, or a Chiaretto del Garda from Italy.

► **M**ake a stir-fry with the same vegetables to serve hot or at room temperature. Dice half an onion and sauté it with the zucchini in 2 tablespoons *each* olive oil and butter. Add the chilis and finally the corn. Season well and transfer to a serving bowl. Garnish in the same way as the soup.

CHICKEN LIVER BARLEY

- [ ] 1 small onion, chopped
- [ ] 6 tablespoons (¾ stick) butter
- [x] 1 cup pearl barley
- [x] 2 cups chicken stock, boiling
- [ ] Salt and black pepper
- [x] ½ pound chicken livers
- [x] ½ pound white mushrooms, sliced

Sauté the onion in half the butter until it is golden. Add the barley and sauté until the grains whiten, about 5 minutes. Add the chicken stock and seasonings, cover the pan tightly, and cook over very low heat for 15 minutes.

Melt the remaining butter in a separate skillet and sauté the chicken livers over high heat until they are browned but still pink inside. Remove the livers and chop them coarsely. Brown the mushrooms quickly in the same pan. Add the mushrooms and livers to the barley, stir well with a fork, and cook, covered, until the barley is tender, 10 to 20 minutes more.

Serve with grilled tomatoes. End with pink grapefruit, doused with Port or Marsala, and broiled.

Y **A** soft, rich red will mix well with the liver, especially St. Emilion or California Merlot. Chianti Classico or Lungarotti's Rubesco would be attractive alternatives from Italy.

► **U**se the same major ingredients with kasha (buckwheat groats) rather than barley. Toast the kasha in an ungreased skillet; then add a beaten egg and stir rapidly until each grain is separate. In a separate skillet, brown the onion and then the mushrooms and livers and add to the kasha, along with the stock and seasonings. Cover tightly and steam for 30 to 40 minutes, or until the grains are *al dente*.

SALSA GRITS

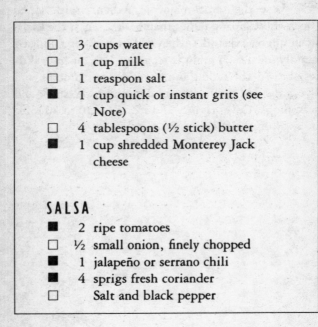

- ☐ 3 cups water
- ☐ 1 cup milk
- ☐ 1 teaspoon salt
- ■ 1 cup quick or instant grits (see Note)
- ☐ 4 tablespoons (½ stick) butter
- ■ 1 cup shredded Monterey Jack cheese

SALSA

- ■ 2 ripe tomatoes
- ☐ ½ small onion, finely chopped
- ■ 1 jalapeño or serrano chili
- ■ 4 sprigs fresh coriander
- ☐ Salt and black pepper

Bring the water and milk to boil in a saucepan. Add the salt and stir in the grits. Lower the heat and simmer until the grits are thick, about 5 minutes. Stir in the butter and cheese.

To make the salsa, broil the tomatoes, turning them to char the skin on all sides. Purée them, skin and all, in a blender. Remove the stem, seeds, and veins of the chili and mince the flesh. Chop the coriander. Mix all ingredients together and taste for seasoning. Make a well in the cooked grits and pour in the salsa.

● **G**ood with steamed asparagus or sautéed string beans.

🍷 **C**hoose a dry, easy red with some zest: inexpensive Zinfandel, a Côtes du Ventoux, or Valpolicella.

▶ **T**o make fried grits, cook the grits the night before. Spread them in a pan and chill. Cut in ½-inch slices; then dip in beaten egg and fresh bread crumbs mixed with grated Parmesan cheese and fry the slices in butter. Pass the salsa in a bowl.

Note: If you can find old-fashioned stoneground grits, prepare them as quick grits, but increase the cooking time to 45 to 60 minutes.

COMPANIONS

YOGURT RICE

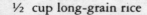

- ■ ½ cup long-grain rice
- ■ 1 small hot pepper, minced
- ■ 2 or 3 slices gingerroot, peeled and minced
- ☐ ½ teaspoon cardamom seeds, crushed
- ☐ ⅛ teaspoon cumin seeds
- ☐ ½ garlic clove, minced
- ☐ 1 tablespoon vegetable oil
- ■ ½ cup yogurt
- ☐ Salt and black pepper
- ☐ 1 tablespoon chopped fresh coriander

Wash the rice in a strainer under cold running water until the water runs clear. Bring 2 quarts of salted water to a boil, add the rice, and boil rapidly for 10 to 12 minutes, or until the rice is tender and softer than *al dente*.

Meanwhile, heat the hot pepper, ginger, cardamom, cumin, and garlic in the oil for 2 to 3 minutes and beat into the yogurt. Season with salt and pepper to taste. When the rice is done, drain it well and toss it with the yogurt. Garnish with the coriander. Serve at any temperature.

NUTTED WILD RICE

- ■ ½ cup wild rice
- ☐ ¾ cup boiling water
- ☐ 2 tablespoons (¼ stick) butter
- ☐ Salt and black pepper
- ■ ⅓ cup toasted pine nuts

Wash the rice in a sieve under cold running water until the water runs clear, about 2 minutes. Drain and put the rice with the boiling water and 1 teaspoon of the butter into the top of a double boiler. Add salt and pepper to taste, cover, and steam over boiling water for 45 to 55 minutes. Mix with the remaining butter and the pine nuts.

Note: Wild rice is excellent cold, as a salad. If you intend to serve it cold, substitute walnut oil for the butter.

GARLIC ROAST POTATOES

- ☒ 1 pound new potatoes
- ☐ 6 garlic cloves
- ☒ 2 sprigs fresh rosemary, or 1 teaspoon dried
- ☐ Salt and black pepper
- ☐ 4 tablespoons (½ stick) butter

Wash the potatoes and place them on a large square of aluminum foil. Peel the garlic and add the cloves to the potatoes. Sprinkle with the rosemary leaves and salt and pepper. Dot with the butter. Bring up the edges of the foil to make a sealed packet and bake at 425 degrees for 45 to 50 minutes if the potatoes are medium size, 25 to 30 minutes if they are small. Keep the potatoes hot in the packet until ready to serve.

SWEET POTATO
STIR-FRY

- ■ 1 small sweet potato
- ☐ 1 small onion, thinly sliced
- ■ 1 sweet red pepper, sliced length-wise
- ☐ 4 tablespoons (½ stick) butter
- ■ 1 tart apple (Granny Smith)
- ☐ 1 tablespoon lemon juice
- ☐ ¼ teaspoon mace
- ☐ Salt and black pepper

Boil the sweet potato in its skin until barely tender. Peel and slice; then cut the slices into strips. Sauté the onion and red pepper in the butter. Peel, core, and slice the apple and add it to the onion. Add the sweet potato and seasonings, sauté quickly over high heat, and serve.

BROCCOLI AND CAULIFLOWERETS

- ■ ½ small head broccoli
- ■ ½ small head cauliflower
- ☐ ½ small dried chili pepper, crushed
- ☐ ½ teaspoon mustard seeds
- ☐ ¼ teaspoon cardamom seeds, crushed
- ☐ ⅛ teaspoon mace
- ☐ Salt and black pepper
- ■ ¼ cup sesame oil

Cut the flowerets of the broccoli and cauliflower from their stems. (Reserve the stems for another purpose, such as soup.) Mix the spices together. Put the vegetables in a steamer (or in a colander set in a pot of boiling water with a lid), sprinkle on the spices, cover, and steam for 5 to 7 minutes until tender but crisp. Transfer to a serving platter and dribble the oil over the top.

ZUCCHINI
GRATIN

- ■ 1 pound small zucchini
- □ 2 tablespoons olive oil
- ■ ½ cup wheat germ
- □ ½ teaspoon dried oregano
- □ Salt, black pepper, and cayenne pepper

Remove the stem ends of the zucchini but leave the skins on. Shred in a processor. Add 1 teaspoon of salt and let the zucchini drain for 10 minutes. Rinse and pat dry with paper towels. Put in a shallow buttered baking pan and sprinkle with the olive oil, wheat germ, and seasonings. Bake at 450 degrees for 15 minutes. Serve at any temperature.

Sesame Eggplant

- ■ 2 Chinese eggplants (long and narrow)
- ■ ½ cup sesame seeds
- ☐ ¼ cup olive oil
- ☐ Salt and black pepper

Cut off the stem ends of the eggplants. Cut lengthwise into quarters or eighths and then in half to make eggplant fingers. Sprinkle with salt and let drain for 10 minutes.

Meanwhile, toast the sesame seeds in a 375-degree oven for 5 to 8 minutes. Remove. Raise the oven temperature to 450 degrees. Pat the eggplant dry with paper towels, sprinkle them with pepper, and roll them quickly in the olive oil. Put them in a baking pan and bake for 8 to 10 minutes, or until just tender. Coat with the sesame seeds and serve.

PEARS IN CHINESE HOT SAUCE

- ■ 2 firm Bosc pears
- ■ ½ small hot red pepper
- ☐ ½ garlic clove, minced
- ■ 2 slices gingerroot, peeled and shredded
- ■ 2 tablespoons sesame oil

Quarter and peel the pears and cut into thick slices. Sauté the pepper, garlic, and gingerroot in the oil for 2 to 3 minutes. Add the pears and brown them quickly on both sides. A good accompaniment for roast birds or pork.

AFTERWARDS

Margarita Oranges

■ 2 navel oranges
□ 2 tablespoons powdered sugar
■   Juice of 2 limes
■ 2 tablespoons tequilla
■ 1½ tablespoons Cointreau or
        Triple Sec

Peel the oranges and section them. Sprinkle with the sugar, lime juice, Tequilla, and Cointreau, cover with plastic wrap, and refrigerate until ready to serve.

Or you can macerate the peeled and sliced oranges in rose water or fresh orange juice and sprinkle them with cinnamon.

Any good sweet muscat is the perfect complement to oranges: Muscat Beaumes de Venise from the Rhône, California Muscat (try Quady's "Essencia"), or an Italian Moscato.

WALNUT-APRICOT TART

- ☒ 1 cup dried apricots, chopped
- ☒ ⅓ cup dark rum
- ☒ ¾ cup walnuts
- ☐ ¾ cup flour
- ☒ ¾ cup brown sugar
- ☐ 6 tablespoons (¾ stick) butter, melted
- ☐ 3 eggs, beaten
- ☐ ¼ cup honey
- ☐ 1 teaspoon vanilla
- ☐ Cinnamon and whipped cream

Soak the apricots in the rum while making the crust. Coarsely grind the walnuts in a processor and mix half of them with the flour, sugar, and butter. Press the mixture onto the bottom and sides of a 9-inch pie pan. Sprinkle with the remaining walnuts.

Beat together the apricots, rum, eggs, honey, and vanilla. Pour the mixture into the crust and bake at 350 degrees for 30 to 40 minutes, or until the eggs are set. Sprinkle with cinnamon and serve with cream.

California late harvest Rieslings are good with apricots, but Sauternes, Rhine Auslese, or an Alsatian Vendange Tardive would also work well.

BLACKENED FIGS

- ½ pound dried figs
- 3 cups red wine
- ½ cup honey
- ½ cup port

Put figs in a deep baking dish and cover with the red wine and honey. Bake at 350 degrees for 60 minutes. (The figs will absorb most of the liquid and turn almost black in color.) Pour the port over the figs and stir to dissolve the remaining liquid. Serve by themselves or with vanilla ice cream.

If the figs are served alone, try a California Muscat, Italian Moscato, or Muscat Beaumes de Venise.

MAPLE TOFFEE APPLES OR PEARS

- ■ 2 firm pears or apples
- □ 2 tablespoons lemon juice
- □ 3 tablespoons butter
- ■ 2 tablespoons brown sugar
- ■ ¼ cup maple syrup
- ■ ¼ cup heavy cream
- □ 1 teaspoon vanilla
- □ ⅓ cup toasted chopped pecans

Quarter, core, peel, and slice the apples or pears and sprinkle them with the lemon juice.

Make a sauce by melting 1 tablespoon of the butter with the brown sugar, maple syrup, and cream in a saucepan. Boil the sauce, stirring, for 4 to 5 minutes, or until it thickens. Remove from the heat and add the vanilla.

In a heavy skillet, fry the fruit slices in the remaining butter over high heat to cook them slightly but not until they are limp. Pour the sauce over them and sprinkle with the pecans.

An Auslese from the Mosel will match both the richness of the sauce and the particular flavors of pears and apples. Sauternes would also be appropriate.

AVOCADO-PINEAPPLE CREAM

- ■ 1 ripe avocado
- ■ 1 lime
- ■ ½ fresh pineapple
- □ 2 to 3 tablespoons honey
- ■ 2 tablespoons Kirsch or other fruit brandy

Cut the avocado into quarters, peel, and put the flesh into a processor or blender. Grate the rind of the lime and add it to the avocado with the juice of the lime.

Cut the pineapple half in two, lengthwise. Remove the center core and slice the flesh crosswise; then cut the flesh from the rind as if cutting off a melon rind. Add the pineapple slices, honey, and Kirsch to the avocado and purée until smooth. Taste and add more lime or honey accordingly.

Scoop the purée into a metal pan (to conduct cold) and put in the freezer until ready to serve. If the cream is frozen hard, spoon it into a processor and whip it again into a purée; then serve.

Avocado is not a suitable match for most wines, but a sparkling dessert wine, like a Champagne Doux or an Asti Spumante, would do fine.

FROZEN CHOCOLATE TRUFFLE

- ■ 3 ounces bittersweet chocolate (Lindt is best)
- ☐ 1 tablespoon strong espresso coffee (or Medaglio d'Oro Instant)
- ☐ 6 tablespoons (¾ stick) butter, cut into 6 slices
- ■ 2 tablespoons Cognac or Grand Marnier
- ☐ 2 eggs, separated
- ☐ 2 tablespoons superfine sugar
- ■ ¼ cup hazelnuts, toasted and finely chopped

Melt the chocolate with the coffee in the top of a double boiler over simmering water. Beat in the butter, remove from the heat, and add the Cognac.

Beat the egg yolks with the sugar until thick. Beat the egg whites until stiff but not dry.

Beat the chocolate mixture into the egg yolks. Fold in the whites, sprinkle the top with the nuts, and put in the freezer until ready to serve.

♈ There *is* a wine that can be happily consumed with chocolate: California port (look for Quady or Ficklin) or, better yet, a late harvest Zinfandel.

FRESH FRUIT MACEDONIA

- ■ 1 cup *each* strawberries, cherries, plums, red grapes, and blueberries
- ☐ 1 lemon
- ☐ 2 tablespoons honey
- ■ 1 tablespoon crème de cassis
- ■ ½ cup port
- ☐ ¼ teaspoon ground cinnamon
- ☐ ¼ cup shelled pistachios

Hull the strawberries, pit the cherries, and stone the plums, cutting them into quarters if they are large. If the grapes have seeds, cut the grapes in half and remove the seeds. Grate the lemon rind and mix with the honey, cassis, port, and cinnamon.

Put the fruit in a serving bowl, pour the liquid over it, cover with a plastic wrap, and refrigerate until ready to serve. Sprinkle the pistachios over the top before serving.

An Alsatian Gewürztraminer Vendange Tardive will provide the right balance between sweetness and spice, though a Tawny Port or Banyuls could be enjoyed as well.

CONCERNING THE WINE

When you're shopping for wine, no book or vintage chart can help you as much as a retailer you trust. Find a serious wine shop—one with plenty of bottles to choose from in each category of vintage, price range, and type. Look for exotica, not so much to buy as for a sign of expertise; any shop able to obtain such rare (and expensive) California wineries as Mount Eden, Chalone, Mayacamas, Diamond Creek, or Matanzas Creek is likely to be a serious enterprise.

Then, if the diversity bewilders you, ask for help. The best merchants will be eager to give recommendations without being pushy, will freely admit whether or not they have tasted the wine you're interested in, will be outspoken in their opinion of it, and will usually be able to steer you to a less expensive, often lesser known, alternative.

Once you've located a reliable merchant, you can help him out in turn by knowing how much you need (figure six generous glasses to the bottle), what you're serving for dinner, any preferences you might have (red or white, sweet or dry, light or full-bodied), and how much you wish to spend. Though good wines can often be found for less than five dollars a bottle, a greater range of possibilities opens up between five and ten dollars. And for the best wine, ten to twenty should bring you all but the very finest Champagne, Burgundy, Bordeaux, or Vintage Port. Be sensible, but be adventurous as well, open to suggestion and, from time to time, a little indulgent.

One bottle will usually suffice for a meal for two, but what about something to sip before or after? Half-bottles are useful in this regard, as are sweeter wines, which (thanks to their sugar content) will keep for a day or two in the fridge without fading: the sweeter varieties of California whites (especially those designated "Late Harvest"), Sauternes, Vouvray, German and Alsatian wines, and Hungarian Tokay, are all possibilities. Fortified wines are another solution: before dinner, a cold fino sherry (Tio Pepe or Duff Gordon) can be lovely, while port is a classic with Stilton cheese and apples after dinner (Sandeman's "Founder's Reserve" is an excellent choice with a modest price tag).

Port, of course, should never be chilled. In fact, the only respectable red that *should* be chilled is Beaujolais. On the other hand, the flavor of red wine goes flat if it's not slightly cooler than "room temperature"; an easy solution is to put any bottle of red wine in the fridge for 10 minutes before serving. Remember that sweet whites should always be served very cold, whereas the drier varieties, especially white Burgundies and other fine Chardonnays, should be only moderately chilled.

Do not cook with anything less than a good generic red or white—for example, Mondavi or Boucheron—or, better yet, use what's left from last night's dinner wine.

One all-purpose wineglass will suit most types, as long as it's large (10 to 12 ounces) and wide enough to swirl the contents (a practical way of releasing the scent); a round or tulip-shaped bowl about three inches across the rim is ideal. For sparkling wines, use a "flute" if possible, which is better designed for conserving the bubbles than the traditional type of Champagne glass with the shallow bowl. Never use tinted or opaque glasses, which make it impossible to enjoy the color of the wine.

Older red wines with sediment should be poured into a decanter so the bitter "dregs" don't mar the taste. Sediment, by the way, is not a bad sign, but an indication that the wine is mature.

What follows is a brief and by no means exhaustive listing of wines that can be relied on to offer the best values in their respective regions. Bear in mind that the strategies for identifying good value vary with the idiosyncracies of each region, so that, for instance, an importer's name may sometimes give a better clue to quality than the name of the vineyard itself.

Nearly all these recommendations should provide good wines for less, often considerably less, than twenty dollars a bottle. If you are interested in a good comprehensive guide that includes the more expensive and illustrious estates, nothing compares for concision and common sense with Hugh Johnson's *Pocket Encyclopedia of Wine.*

Finally, the suggestions offered here, including the recommendations that accompany the recipes, are merely that: suggestions. Whenever you're assembling your own wine list for the most intimate restaurant in town, the best guide is always your own palate.

BURGUNDY is the most expensive of all wines and the most complex to study. Nevertheless, the reds can be the most intensely flavored of all, while the whites set the standard for dry white wine. The greatest vineyards for white wine are located in *Puligny-Montrachet, Chassagne-Montrachet,* and *Meursault,* while the best reds usually come from such towns as *Gevrey-Chambertin*, *Chambolle-Musigny*, and *Vosne-Romanée*. Good wines in a more affordable price range, however, often bear the names *Fixin, Savigny, Pernand-Vergelesses, Santenay, Mercurey, Auxey-Duresses,* and *Rully*. As a rule of thumb, quality has more to do with the name of the grower, *negociant,* or importer than with the name of the wine itself. These are some of the better names in each category:

Importers: Chadderdon; Kermit Lynch; Vineyard Brands; World Shippers; Wildman; Schoonmaker; Select Vineyards; Canaan & Wasserman / Europvin.
Negociants: Faiveley; Bourée; Drouhin; Jadot; Clair-Daü; Bruck; Latour (whites only); Moillard; Merode.
Red Burgundy Growers: Jayer; Arnoux; Pousse d'Or; Rion; Amiot; Noellat; Chevillon; Dujac; Morot; Ponsot; Rousseau.
White Burgundy Growers: Comtes Lafon; Boillot; Leflaive; Roulot; Bachelet; Morey; Rapet; Ampeau; Michelot-Buisson; Michelot-Garnier.

BORDEAUX is the home of scores of celebrated châteaus, including such glamorous names as Petrus, Lafite-Rothschild, d'Yquem, Margaux, Latour, and Haut-Brion. The trick, of course, is finding estates that are first-rate, reasonably priced, and don't require twenty years of bottle age. The reds of *St. Emilion* and *Pomerol* tend to be softer, fuller, and simpler than the more classical *Médocs* and *Graves*. *Graves* also produces fine, somewhat austere dry whites, while *Sauternes* and *Barsac* are famous for dessert whites that are fabulously rich and sweet. Here the information crucial to selection is the name of the château itself.

Red Médocs and Graves: La Lagune; Calon-Ségur; Bran-aire-Ducru; du Tertre; Haut-Batailley; Grand-Puy-Ducasse; Cantemerle; Meyney; Talbot; Gloria; Prieuré-Lichine; Chasse-Spleen; Potensac; de Pez; Fourcas-Hosten; Haut-Marbuzet; Lanessan; Ramage-la-Batisse; Sociando-Mallet; Haut-Bailly; Pape-Clément; La Louvière; Rahoul; Coufran; Poujeaux; Larose-Trintaudon; Greysac. Château Laurétan is a good wine under five dollars.

Red St. Emilion and Pomerol: Belair; L'Arrosée; Bon Pasteur; Clos René; Certan-Guiraud; Clos des Jacob-ins; Soutard; Clos Plince; Monbousquet; La Domi-nique; Petit-Village.

White Graves: La Louvière; Couhins; Rahoul; Millet; Carbonnieux.

Sauternes & Barsac: Coutet; Rieussec; Suduiraut; Doisy-Daëne; Doisy-Védrines; Fargues; Raymond-Lafon; Nairac; Caillou; Haut-Peyraguey.

RHÔNE wines tend to be powerful, full-flavored, and moderately priced. *Hermitage, Côte-Rôtie,* and *Châteauneuf-du-Pape* are the great names, but good values can be had for less from *Saint-Joseph, Cornas, Vacqueyras,* and *Gigondas. Côtes du Rhône* from a good producer can often be a terrific buy, as well as *Côtes du Ventoux* (look for Vieille Ferme).

Top Rhône Producers: Guigal; Beaucastel; Jaboulet Ainé; Chapoutier; Jasmin; Chave; Clape; Vidal-Fleury; Guy de Barjac; Meffre.

CHAMPAGNE: The genuine article is always from France. Among the best producers of the more full-bodied style are Veuve Clicquot, Bollinger, Roederer,

Pol Roger, Krug, and Barancourt. If you like the lighter, crisper style, look for Perrier-Jouet, Deutz, Billecart-Salmon, Charbaut, and Taittinger. The famous "luxury blends," such as Dom Pérignon and Roederer Cristal, are an extravagance.

LOIRE, CHABLIS: After good French *Chablis* (bearing the classifications "Grand Cru" or "Premier Cru" on the label), the best mates for shellfish are the tart, pungent whites from *Sancerre* and *Pouilly-Fumé*, though the lighter, less expensive *Muscadet* is just as suitable. *Vouvray* and *Anjou* make delightful sweet and semisweet whites, perfect for dessert or aperitifs. Also try the fine, delicate sparkling wines from firms such as Monmousseau, Bouvet, and Gratien & Meyer, which sell for considerably less than true *Champagne*.

Chablis Producers: Moreau; Regnard; Raveneau; Fèvre.
Loire Producers: Sauvion; Barre; Gaudry; Reverdy; Auvigue; Rémy-Pannier; Burrier; Chereau.

ALSACE: Good Alsatian *Gewürztraminer*, whether made dry or sweet, is a wine of great character and a favorite of connoisseurs. The dry version is a useful match for the spicier foods that tend to clash with other good wines. The sweeter wines are usually called "Vendange Tardive." Willm, Weinbach, Hugel, and Trimbach are four top producers.

GERMANY: The finer sweet wines are incomparable for their combination of sweetness, delicacy, spectacular flavor, and flowery aroma. Always buy bottles labeled "Qualitätswein mit Prädikat," which will carry designations indicating the ascending levels of sweetness (Kabinett, Spätlese, Auslese, followed by the rare and expensive Beerenauslese and Trockenbeerenauslese). *Mosel* wines tend to be crisper, lighter, and more flowery than their richer counterparts from the *Rhine*. *Mosel* comes in a green bottle; *Rhine* comes in amber. Check Hugh Johnson for descriptions of specific vineyards.

Some Good Producers: Basserman-Jordan; Bürklin-Wolf; Schloss Vollrads; von Plettenberg; Staatsweingut; Schloss Schönborn; Egon Müller; von Simmern; Prüm; Guntrum; von Bühl.

ITALY: The useful whites, including *Pinot Grigio, Orvieto, Vernacchia,* and *Frascati,* are overshadowed by the reds, which are various and often very good. *Chianti Classico* is a versatile companion to all sorts of foods (look for Monsanto, Ruffino, and Antinori among others), while the more aggressive reds made in the Piedmont region from the Nebbiolo grape can challenge the best of France and California. The best of these are *Barolo* and *Barbaresco,* but less expensive examples are *Spanna, Gattinara, Ghemme,* and *Inferno. Dolcetto* and *Nebbiolo d'Alba* are good lighter reds. Also look for the newer wines now being made from French grapes, such as Cabernet, Merlot, and Chardonnay.

Some Good Producers in the Piedmont: Brugo; Ceretto; Conterno; Pio Cesare; Dessilani; Vallana; Einaudi; Fontanafredda; Giacosa; Mascarello; Prunotto; Ratti; Rinaldi; Vietti.

SPAIN is best known for good cheap sparkling wines, such as those from Codorniu, and for fine reds. A traditional favorite is the elegant, full-flavored wine of *Rioja* (look for Paternina, CUNE, Tondonia, Lopez Heredia, Cerro Anon, and the three Marqués wines: Murrieta, Caceres, and Riscale). Terrific Cabernets comparable to fine Bordeaux are being made by the more modern firms of Torres and Jean León.

CALIFORNIA: Top wineries comparable to the best include Phelps, Carneros Creek, Burgess, Rutherford Hill, Clos du Bois, Dehlinger, Simi, Mondavi, Beringer, Franciscan, and Raymond. Raymond, especially, stands out as an exceptional value in nearly every category. Specialists in good reds include Ridge, Stag's Leap Winery, BV, Caymus, Clos du Val, Conn Creek, Dry Creek, and Rafanelli. For whites, look for Acacia, Landmark, Felton Empire, and Sonoma-Cutrer. Closer to the five-dollar range, Parducci, Sebastiani, Fetzer, Round Hill, Roudon-Smith, and Sutter Home are all trustworthy names. For sparkling wines, Iron Horse, Domaine Chandon, Piper-Sonoma, and Korbel are four wineries which consistently offer good values.

Also look for the up-and-coming wineries of **OREGON**, where some of the best Pinot Noir, Riesling, and Chardonnay you can buy are being produced and, all too often, overlooked. Some wineries to look for: Eyrie, Elk Cove, Knudsen-Erath, Sokol-Blosser, Amity, Adelsheim, and Peter Adams. For well-made wines from **NEW YORK**, look for Wagner, Glenora, Hargrave, Lenz, and Bridgehampton.

Last of all, AUSTRALIA is becoming a popular source for alternatives to California. Wineries to seek out include Rosemount, Penfold's, Petaluma, Taltarni, Peter Lehman, and Johnstone.

—William Wadsworth

WINE NOTES

_____

_____

_____

_____

_____

_____

_____

_____

_____

WINE NOTES

_____

_____

_____

_____

_____

_____

_____

_____

_____

WINE NOTES

WINE NOTES

WINE NOTES 🍷

_____

_____

_____

_____

_____

_____

_____

_____

_____

WINE NOTES 🍷

_____

_____

_____

_____

_____

_____

_____

_____

_____

WINE NOTES

_____

_____

_____

_____

_____

_____

_____

_____

_____

WINE NOTES

_____

_____

_____

_____

_____

_____

_____

_____

_____

WINE NOTES

_____

_____

_____

_____

_____

_____

_____

_____

_____

WINE NOTES

_____

_____

_____

_____

_____

_____

_____

_____

_____

_____

INDEX